The Cynic's Dictionary

The Cynic's Dictionary

Aubrey Dillon-Malone

CONTEMPORARY BOOKS

Cover design by Bob Eames
Cover image by Hulton Getty

This edition of *The Cynic's Dictionary* is published under
license from Prion Books Limited, London.

This edition first published in 2000 by Contemporary Books
A division of NTC/Contemporary Publishing Group, Inc.
4255 West Touhy Avenue, Lincolnwood (Chicago), Illinois
60712-1975 U.S.A.
Copyright © 1998 Aubrey Dillon Malone
Printed in Great Britain
International Standard Book Number: 0-8092-2546-8
00 01 02 03 04 CPD 14 13 12 11 10 9 8 7 6 5 4 3 2 1

Introduction

YOUR AVERAGE DICTIONARY may well be a *sine qua non* if you wish to access the received lexicographical wisdom, but as Ambrose Bierce demonstrated with his wickedly acerbic *Devil's Dictionary* – well represented in these pages – words don't always behave themselves as we might ideally like them to behave.

This isn't to say that dictionaries don't tell it like it is. They do if one assumes that two and two are always four, and that the shortest distance between two points is always a straight line. However, as Mae West once observed, "a curve is the loveliest distance between two points." *The Cynic's Dictionary* is a book which exploits that curve at some length. And with not a little malice.

This cynical curve is more often than not a deeply humorous one and a more honorable and pleasurable manner of assessing reality than dourness ever was. The Irish poet Paddy Kavanagh once described tragedy as undeveloped comedy—he had a point. And of course the opposite is also true. Bishop Whately said that happiness is no laughing matter. Neither is comedy.

I have attempted to straddle a middle ground between this Scylla and Charybdis, collecting quotations from all eras and continents which emphasize the pitiful manner in which language all too often fails to measure up to life, love, and the whole damn thing – either because of evasive euphemism or downright tunnel vision.

Agatha Christie defined speech as an "invention of man's to keep him from thinking." Joseph Conrad went

further, describing words as "the great foes of reality." It is the ambition of this book to try and give some of our words back their dignity by exposing the fraudulence of their dictionary definitions.

In the best of all possible worlds, *Webster's Dictionary* would have obviated the need for Ambrose Bierce's one, or this, but when we consider the fact that words, like anything else, are only as good or as bad as the person using them, then some kind of etymological do-it-yourself kit must be assembled to stop them getting away with murder in unchecked environments.

As Alice in Wonderland emoted, words often mean what we *want* them to mean, and this can have disastrous repercussions on both speakers and auditors alike when one is being mendaciously diplomatic. The people featured in this book would hardly be taken in by such doublethink, or doublespeak, and I'm pleased to share their wisdom, jaundiced as it is, with any readers these pages will find.

In many ways, the book is an homage to Mr. Bierce, and if he appears to be over-represented, then perhaps that's a reflection on the fact that nobody has bettered his serendipitous approach to life since he first began penning entries in 1869 for what would eventually be called *The Devil's Dictionary.* Apart from the redoubtable Bierce, I have drawn heavily on the works of many other great cynics and satirists—Oscar Wilde, George Bernard Shaw, Mark Twain, Herbert Prochnow, H.L. Mencken, Elbert Hubbard and a number of other luminaries who will be household names to those of us who have a

penchant for epigrammatic wit. Even Dr. Johnson, the great lexicographer himself, is in there. Renowned for his generous wit he even managed to included a scattering of cynical definitions in his original *Dictionary of the English Language*. The entry for "oats," for instance, read—"a grain which in England is generally given to horses, but in Scotland supports the people."

The aforementioned Henry Louis Mencken, who, as a journalist in the first half of the twentieth century editing the *Smart Set* and the *American Mercury* (with an acid pen to match that of Bierce's), defined a cynic as "somebody who, when he smells flowers, looks for a coffin." And if we accept Edith Summerskill's definition of nagging as "the repetition of unpalatable truths" then maybe we're entitled to say that cynics have had a bad press through the ages.

The cynic is defined in the "real" dictionary as "a person who always believes the worst" but Bierce's devilish definition is far more true to the original sense of the word: "a blackguard whose faulty vision sees things as they are, and not how they ought to be." Cynicism as a philosophy, in the hands of its ancient Greek founders – Diogenes and Antisthenes – sprang not from unfounded antagonism but from disappointed and disillusioned idealism. Seen in this light the cynic becomes a person who has the moral (and politically incorrect) courage to lay the cupboard bare and say, once again, that the emperor has no clothes. If this is the case, then the real devils aren't so much Mr. Bierce and yours truly after all, but those who would seek to browbeat and brainwash us with bromides, sugar-coating the bitter pill of a murky reality with fashionable anodynes.

Much of the humor produced by our poor cynics then can be seen as ultimately not malicious but defensive. As Lambert Jeffries put it, a cynic is in fact "a sentimentalist afraid of himself," and as Arland Ussher once said, his humour is really "despair refusing to take itself seriously." Much of the cynicism on show here – in the spirit of the original sense of the world – is sublimely subversive. Yet to leaven the brew, I've found room for a good measure of downright idiotic cynicism – something old Diogenes (who lived for most of his life naked in a barrel, and had a penchant for answering questions not with words but a sharp blast of flatulence) was a master of himself.

If devils we are, Mr. Bierce and I, we're well-intentioned ones, and we make it our mission to bring down only the high-minded, pretentious and pietistic. As the man said, "Give me heaven for the climate and hell for the company." That's my excuse anyway.

Finally, most anthologists of quotations, according to the French 18th-century cynic and wit, Nicolas-Sebastien Chamfort, "are like those who eat cherries – first picking the best ones and winding up by eating everything." With the invaluable assistance of my editor Andrew Goodfellow I have endeavoured to avoid this temptation, retaining only the pick of the crop.

Aubrey Dillon-Malone

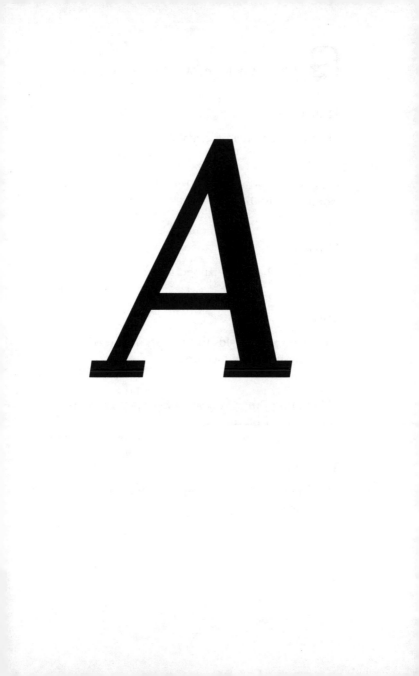

Ability

The ability to *conceal* one's ability.

Duc de la Rochefoucauld

The art of getting credit for all the home runs someone else hits.

Casey Stengal

Abroad

That large home of ruined reputations.

George Eliot

Abstainer

A person who yields to the temptation of denying himself a pleasure.

Ambrose Bierce

The kind of man you wouldn't want to drink with even if he did.

George Jean Nathan

Absurdity

A statement of belief manifestly inconsistent with one's own opinion.

Ambrose Bierce

The Cynic's Dictionary

Accidents

Fate misnamed.

Napoleon

Accountancy

The closest to hell I've ever been.

Chris Blackwell

Acting

The most minor of gifts, and not a very high class way to earn a living. After all, Shirley Temple could do it at the age of four.

Katharine Hepburn

A good training for political life. The only problem is the speeches are harder to learn.

Ronald Reagan

A way of living out one's insanity.

Isabelle Huppert

Standing up naked and turning round very slowly.

Rosalind Russell

Farting about in disguise.

Peter O'Toole

Action

The last resource of those who know not how to dream.

Oscar Wilde

Actions

What lie louder than words.

Carolyn Wells

Actor

Someone who can remember his briefest notice well into senescence, long after he has forgotten his phone number or where he lives.

Anon.

A guy who if you ain't talkin' about him, he ain't listening.

Marlon Brando

A ghost looking for a body to inhabit.

Gall Godwin

Actors

The only honest hypocrites.

William Hazlitt

People who should be treated like cattle.

Alfred Hitchcock

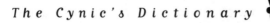
People who should keep their mouths shut and hope for the best.

Richard Burton

Actress

Someone with no ability who waits to go on alimony.

Jackie Stallone

Actuary

Someone who cannot stand the excitement of chartered accountancy.

Glan Thomas

Adam

The luckiest man in the world – because he had no mother-in-law.

Sholom Aleichem

Addresses

Items given to us to conceal our whereabouts.

Saki

Adolescence

The period in a kid's life when parents become difficult.

Ryan O'Neal

 *The Cynic's Dictionary*

The period of life between puberty and adultery.

Kevin Goldstein-Jackson

The age at which children stop asking questions because they know all the answers.

Jeanne Opalach

Adolescents

People who never seem to realise that one day they will be as dumb as their parents.

Revd James Simpson

People whose job it is to turn on you.

Ron Howard

Adult

One who has ceased to grow vertically but not horizontally.

Kevin Goldstein-Jackson

A child blown up by age.

Simone de Beauvoir

Adultery

A stimulant to men, but a sedative to women.

Malcolm de Chazal

The application of democracy to love.

H.L. Mencken

Advertising

Legalised lying.

H.G. Wells

The greatest art form of the 20th century.

Marshall McLuhan

The most truthful part of a newspaper.

Thomas Jefferson

The cheapest way of selling goods, particularly if they're worthless.

Sinclair Lewis

The rattling of a stick inside a swill bucket.

George Orwell

The most fun you can have with your clothes on.

Jerry Della Femina

The art of making whole lies out of half-truths.

Edgar A. Shoaff

Advertising Agency

Eighty-five per cent confusion and 15 per cent commission.

Fred Allen

Advice

Something delicately poised between cliché and indiscretion.

Archbishop Robert Runcie

What we ask for when we already know the answer, but wish we didn't.

Erica Jong

Age

Something a woman conceals because a man rarely acts his.

Leopold Fechtner

Alcohol

What makes the tart grow fonder.

Addison Mizner

A very necessary article. It enables Parliament to do things at eleven at night that no sane man would do at eleven in the morning.

George Bernard Shaw

A liquid effective for preserving everything –
except secrets.

Henny Youngman

Alcoholic

Someone who suffers from bottle fatigue.

Louis Safian

Anyone you don't like who drinks more than
you do.

Dylan Thomas

Alcoholism

Not a spectator sport, because eventually the
whole family gets to play.

Joyce Rebeta-Burdett

The one disease which tells you you don't have
a problem.

Honor Heffernan

Alimony

The ransom the happy pay to the devil.

H.L. Mencken

Billing minus cooing.

Mary Dorsey

The wages of sin.

Audrey Austin

What makes you realise how short a month is.

John Barrymore

Alone

In bad company.

Ambrose Bierce

Amateur

One who accepts cash rather than cheques.

Jack Kelly

Ambassador

An honest man sent abroad to lie for the Commonwealth.

Sir Henry Wooton

Ambition

An overmastering desire to be vilified by enemies while living, and made ridiculous by friends when dead.

Ambrose Bierce

Avarice on stilts.

Samuel Johnson

The last refuge of the failure.

Oscar Wilde

A way of working yourself to death to live better.

Brendan Behan

America

A country where you can buy a lifetime supply of aspirin for a dollar, and use it up in two weeks.

John Barrymore

A mistake, a giant mistake!

Sigmund Freud

One long expectoration.

Oscar Wilde

Like an unfaithful lover who promised us more than we got.

Charlotte Bunch

A country where they lock up juries and let defendants out.

Herbert Prochnow

A country that doesn't know where it's going but is going to break the speed limit to get there.

Laurence Peter

The place where you can say what you think without even thinking.

Anon

Americans

Like rich fathers who wish they knew how to give their sons the hardships that made them rich.

Robert Frost

Amusement

The happiness of those who cannot think.

Alexander Pope

Anniversaries

Like martinis – after a few you don't bother to count them.

Leopold Fechtner

Anthology

What tears the soul out of a work, then labels its squirming parts.

Frank Jennings

Ants

Insects that attend picnics for a living.

Kenny Everett

Good citizens – they place group interests first.

Clarence Day

Antique

Something that has been useless so long, it's still in pretty good condition.

Franklin P. Jones

Apology

Egotism the wrong side out.

Oliver Wendell Holmes Jnr.

The only thing that will allow you to get the last word with a woman.

Danny Cummins

Appeasers

People who believe that if you keep throwing steaks at a tiger, he'll become a vegetarian.

Heywood Broun

One who feeds a crocodile, hoping it will eat him last.

Winston Churchill

Appetisers

Those little bits you eat until you lose your appetite.

Herbert Prochnow

Applause

The custom of showing one's pleasure at beautiful music by immediately following it with ugly noise.

Percy Scholes

Archaeologist

A man whose career is in ruins.

Hal Roach

The best husband a woman can have – the older she gets, the more interested he is in her.

Agatha Christie

Archbishop

A Christian ecclesiastic of a rank superior to that attained by Christ.

H.L. Mencken

Architecture

The art of how to waste space.

Philip Johnston

Argument

When two people are trying to get the last word in first.

Don Rickles

Aristocrat

A democrat gone to seed.

Ralph W. Emerson

Armpits

Parts of the body that lead lives of quiet perspiration.

Anon.

Army

A body of men assembled to rectify the mistakes of the diplomats.

Joseph Daniels

What you join to see the world, meet interesting people – and kill them.

Woody Allen

Arson

An artificial crime because a large number of houses *deserve* to be burnt.

H. G. Wells

Art

The great refusal of the world as it is.
Herbert Marcuse

The apotheosis of solitude.
Hugh Kenner

The artist's false Catholicism, the fake promise
of an afterlife, and just as fake as heaven and
hell.
Woody Allen

Nature speeded up, and God slowed down.
Malcolm de Chazal

Significant deformity.
Roger Fry

A lie that makes us realise the truth.
Pablo Picasso

The reasoned derangement of the senses.
Kenneth Rexroth

What sells.
Frank Lloyd Wright

An attempt to integrate evil.
Simon de Beauvoir

Artist

Someone who must know how to convince
others of the truth of his lies.

Pablo Picasso

Artistic Temperament

A disease that afflicts amateurs.

G.K. Chesterton

Assassination

The most extreme form of censorship.

George Bernard Shaw

Associate Producer

The only kind of person who will associate
with a producer.

Billy Wilder

Astronauts

Rotarians in outer space.

Gore Vidal

Atheism

A crutch for those who can't stand the reality
of God.

Tom Stoppard

 *The Cynic's Dictionary*

Atheist

A guy who watches a Notre Dame versus SMU football game and doesn't care who wins.

Dwight Eisenhower

Somebody with no invisible means of support.

John Buchan

Attic

Where you store junk you'd throw away if you didn't have one.

Herbert Prochnow

Auctioneer

Someone who never lies unless it's absolutely necessary.

Josh Billings

Someone who proclaims with his hammer that he's picked your pocket with his tongue.

Anon.

Audiences

Coughing bastards.

Donald Wolfit

Australia

The only country in the world where the word 'academic' is regularly used as a term of abuse.

Leslie Kramer

Australians

Violently loud alcoholic roughnecks whose idea of fun is to throw up in your car.

P.J. O'Rourke

Authors

People who are easy enough to get on with – if you're fond of children.

Michael Joseph

Like uncaptured criminals, the only people who are free from routine.

Eric Linkletter

Autobiography

An obituary in serial form with the last instalment missing.

Quentin Crisp

Alibi-ography.

Clare Boothe Luce

A book that suggests the only thing wrong
with the author is ...his memory.

Franklin P. Jones

Books that ought to begin with Chapter Two.

Ellery Sedgwick

Unrivalled vehicles for telling the truth – about
others.

Philip Guedalla

What is now as common as adultery – and
hardly less reprehensible.

John Grigg

The life story of a motor car.

Peter Eldin

Avalanches

Things that happen to other people, in the
resorts you never go to.

Mark Heller

Avarice

The spur of industry.

David Hume

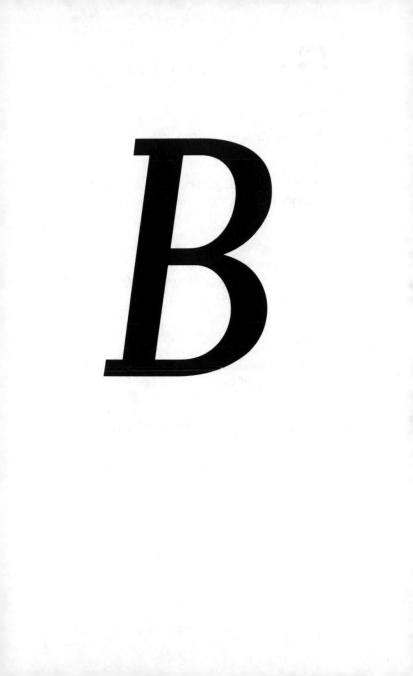

Baby

Nine months interest on a small deposit.

Brian Johnston

A loud noise at one end, and no sense of responsibility at the other.

Ronald Knox

A mis-shapen creature of no particular age, sex or condition, chiefly remarkable for the violence of the sympathies and antipathies it exercises in others.

Ambrose Bierce

Bachelor

A man who never gets over the idea that he's a thing of beauty and a boy for ever.

Helen Rowland

A man who never made the same mistake once.

Anon.

A man who knows that marriage is a device of society designed to make trouble between two people who would otherwise get along very well.

Anthony Quinn

Bachelors

People who never vacuum behind the couch.

Rita Rudner

People who know more about women than
married men; if they didn't, they'd be
married too.

H.L. Mencken

Bank

A place that will lend you money if you
can prove that you don't need it.

Bob Hope

Banker

A man that lends another man the money of a
third man.

Baron Guy de Rosthchild

Barrister

A word in the dictionary that comes between
bankrupt and bastard.

Stephen Phillips

Bastard

Lower class love child.

Tina Spencer Knott

Beard

That ornamental excrement that grows
beneath the chin.

Ben Johnson

Beauty

What a woman has when she looks the same
after washing her face.

Hal Roach

What's in the eye of the beerholder.

W.C. Fields

Beauty Spa

A place where one pays astronomical sums to
be over-exercised and under-fed.

Peg Bracken

Bed

The poor man's opera.

Aldous Huxley

Behavioural Psychology

The science of pulling habits out of rats.

Douglas Busch

Belgium

A country invented by the British to annoy
the French.

Charles de Gaulle

Best-seller

A book which somehow sells well because
it is selling well.

Daniel Boorstin

The gilded tomb of a mediocre talent.

Logan Pearsall Smith

Bible, The

The number one book of the ages, written
by a committee.

Louis B. Mayer

Literature, not dogma.

George Santayana

Biblethumper

Someone who's all preaches and scream.

Louis Safian

Big Sisters

The crabgrass on the lawn of life.

Charles M. Schultz

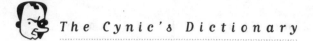

Bigamist

A man who has the bad taste to do what
conscience and the police keep the rest of
us from doing.

Finley Peter Dunne

Bigamy

One way of avoiding the painful publicity
of divorce and the expense of alimony.

Oliver Herford

A case of two rites making a wrong.

Anon.

Having one husband too many.
Monogamy is the same.

Erica Jong

Bigot

One who is obstinately and zealously attached
to an opinion that you do not entertain.

Ambrose Bierce

Bikini

Two bandanas and a worried look.

Leopold Fechtner

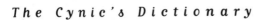

Bimbo

A woman who's not pretty enough to be a model, not smart enough to be an actress, and not nice enough to be a poisonous snake.

P.J. O' Rourke

Biographer

An artist upon oath.

Desmond McCarthy

Biography

Voyeurism embellished with footnotes.

Robert Skidelsky

What ought to be written by an acute enemy.

Arthur James Balfour

Birth

A hereditary disease.

Nigel Rees

The fourth of July of sex.

W.C. Fields

Birthdays

Anniversaries where husbands take a day off, and wives a year off.

Louis Safian

Bisexuality

What doubles your chances of a date on
Saturday night.

Woody Allen

Not so much a cop-out as a fearful
compromise.

Jill Johnston

Blasphemy

The comic verse of belief.

Brendan Behan

Bolshevism

Czarism in overalls.

George Jean Nathan

Book-learning

The dunce's derisive term for all knowledge
that transcends his own impertinent ignorance.

Ambrose Bierce

Book Reviewers

Little old ladies of both sexes.

John O' Hara

Books

Objects that are necessary to correct the vices of the polite.

Oliver Goldsmith

Embalmed minds.

C.N. Bovee

A load of crap.

Philip Larkin

Funny little portable pieces of thought.

Susan Sontag

What they make films out of, for TV.

Robert Morley

Things printed by people who don't understand them, sold by people who don't understand them, read and reviewed by people who don't understand them, and even written by people who don't understand them.

G.C. Lichtenberg

Bop Music

Like playing Scrabble with all the vowels missing.

Duke Ellington

Bore

A fellow who can change the subject back to his topic of conversation faster than you can change it back to yours.

Laurence Peter

A man who, when you ask him how he is, he tells you.

Bert Leston Taylor

Boredom

A vital consideration for the moralist, since at least half the sins of mankind are caused by the fear of it.

Bertrand Russell

Boston

A city with champagne tastes and beer pocketbooks.

Alan Friedberg

A moral and intellectual nursery, always busy applying first principles to trifles.

George Santayana

Botany

The art of insulting flowers in Latin and Greek.

Alphonse Kerr

Boxing

A lot of white men watching two black men beat each other up.

Muhammad Ali

Boy Scout Troop

A lot of boys dressed as jerks, led by a jerk dressed as a boy.

Shelley Berman

Braggart

A guy who enters a conversation feat first.

Tom O' Connor

Brain

Something that starts working the moment you're born and doesn't stop until you stand up to speak in public.

George Jessel

An apparatus with which we think we think.

Ambrose Bierce

An organ that starts working the moment you wake up, and doesn't stop until you get to the office.

Robert Frost

An appendage of the genital glands.

Alexander King

Brandy

A cordial composed of one part thunder and
lightning, one part remorse, two parts bloody
murder, one part death, hell and the grave –
and four parts clarified Satan.

Ambrose Bierce

Brass Bands

Things which are all very well in their place –
outdoors and several miles away.

Thomas Beecham

Bravery

Being the only one who knows you're afraid.

Franklin P. Jones

Brief

A bundle of papers, not in any particular
order, formerly bound in a pink ribbon,
which purports to contain all the information
a barrister needs for the proper running of his
case, but is unlikely to.

Henry Murphy

Britain

A society where the ruling class does not rule, the working class does not work, and the middle class is not in the middle.

George Mikes

British Education

The best in the world – if you can survive it.

Peter Ustinov

British Parliament

The longest running farce in the West End.

Cyril Smith

Broadway

A place where people spend money they haven't earned, to buy things they don't need, to impress people they don't like.

Walter Winchell

The hardened artery of New York.

Walter Winchell

Broker

A man who takes your fortune and turns it into a shoestring.

Alexander Woollcott

Budget

A mathematical confirmation of your worst suspicions.

A.A. Latimer

Bureaucracy

What defends the status quo long after the quo has lost its status.

Laurence Peter

A giant mechanism operated by pygmies.

Honoré de Balzac

Business

Others people's money.

Alexandre Dumas

Businessman

The only man who is forever apologising for his occupation.

H.L. Mencken

Someone judged by the company he keeps... solvent.

Vern McLellan

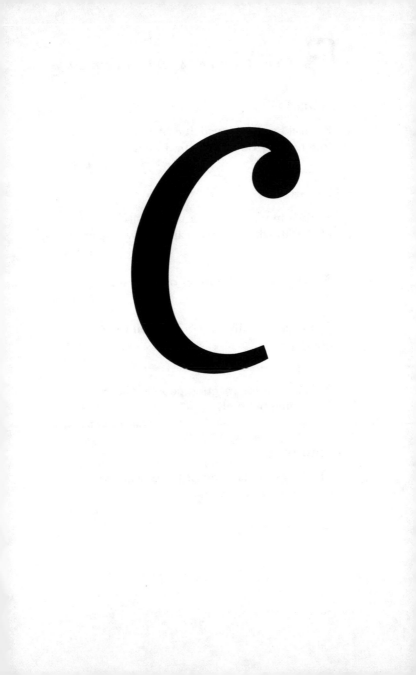

Caddie

A small boy, employed at a liberal stipend, to lose balls for others and find them for himself.

Hal Roach

California

A place in which a boom mentality and a sense of Chekhovian loss meet in uneasy suspension.

Joan Didion

A wet dream in the mind of New York.

Erica Jong

A fine place to live, if you happen to be an orange.

Fred Allen

A great spot for meeting people who come from some place else.

Christopher Isherwood

Californians

The biggest collection of losers who ever met on one piece of real estate.

David Karp

Cambridge

The romantic dream of those who never went there.

Malcolm Muggeridge

Canada

A collection of ten provinces with strong governments loosely connected by fear.

Dave Broadfoot

A country useful only to provide me with furs.

Madame de Pompadour

A country so square that even the female impersonators are women.

Richard Benner

Canadian

A person who knows how to make love in a canoe.

Pierre Berton

A fellow who has become a North American without becoming an American.

Arthur Phelps

Canned music

Audible wallpaper.

Alistair Cooke

Cannibal

Someone fed up with people.

Anon.

Capital

Dead labour which, vampire-like, lives only by sucking living labour, and lives the more, the more labour it sucks.

Karl Marx

Capital Punishment

Killing people who kill people to prove that killing people is wrong.

Sr Helen Prejean

Our society's recognition of the sanctity of human life.

Orrin Hatch

Capitalism

Survival of the fattest.

Anon.

The process whereby American girls turn into American women.

Christopher Hampton

Career

Like the dictionary says, 'A headlong rush, usually downhill'.

Michael Bentine

A wonderful thing, but you can't snuggle up to it on a cold night.

Marilyn Monroe

Caricature

The tribute mediocrity pays to genius.

Oscar Wilde

What shows society, sometimes literally, the arse of history.

William Feaver

Castration

A eunuch experience.

Paul Jennings

Cat

A crossword puzzle with no clues.

Mac O'Brien

A soft, indestructible automaton provided by nature to be kicked when things go wrong in the domestic circle.

Ambrose Bierce

Cats

The fascists of the animal world.

Brian Behan

Catholicism

Good, strong, thick, stupefying incense smoke.

Robert Browning

Catholics

People who take their beliefs *table d'hôte,* unlike Protestants, who take them *à la carte.*

Tom Kettle

Caution

Being dogmatic about tomorrow.

Heywood Broun

Celebrity

A person who is known for his/her well-knownness.

Daniel Boorstin

A person who does nothing for a living, but looks great not doing it.

Julia Phillips

A celebrity is one who is known by many people he is glad he doesn't know.

H.L. Mencken

Any well-known TV or movie star who looks like he spends more than two hours working on his hair.

Steve Martin

A person who works hard all his life to become known, then wears dark glasses to avoid being recognised.

Fred Allen

The advantage of being known by those who don't know you.

Nicolas-Sebastien Chamfort

Celibacy

Not an inherited characteristic.

Nigel Rees

Censor

A man who knows more than he thinks you ought to.

Laurence Peter

Censors

People who are paid to have dirty minds.

John Trevelyan

Censorship

A more depraving and corrupting practice than anything pornography can produce.

Tony Smythe

A legal corollary of public modesty.

Jonathan Miller

An excuse to talk about sex.

Fran Lebowitz

A practice as indefensible as infanticide.

Rebecca West

Censure

The tax a man pays to the public for being eminent.

Jonathan Swift

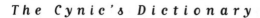

Ceremony

Middle-aged men dressing up like refugees from a pack of cards.

Philip Howard

Certainty

Being mistaken at the top of one's voice.

Ambrose Bierce

Certitude

Servitude.

Jean Rostand

Champagne

A drink that has the taste of an apple peeled with a steel knife.

Aldous Huxley

Chance

Providence's nickname.

Nicolas-Sebastien Chamfort

Chaos

The score upon which reality is written.

Henry Miller

Chappaquiddick

The name of a place brought up by political candidates every time they say they're not going to bring it up.

Mose Russell

Character

What you are in the dark.

Dwight Moody

Charity

The sterilised milk of human kindness.

Oliver Herford

What, like beating, begins at home.

Francis Beaumont

Charm

The ability to get the answer yes without having asked the question.

Albert Camus

Chastity

The most unnatural of the sexual perversions.

Aldous Huxley

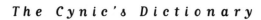

Chatterbox

Someone with a good memory – and a tongue hung in the middle of it.

Louis Safian

Cheese

Milk's leap towards immortality.

Clifton Fadiman

Chess

A game life is too short for.

Henry James Byron

Chicago

Merely a place to change trains.

Jane Byrne

Virgin territory for whorehouses.

Al Capone

Child

A creature that stands halfway between an adult and a TV set.

Herbert Prochnow

Childhood

A series of happy delusions.

Sydney Smith

The time of life when you make faces in a mirror. Middle age is when the mirror gets even!

Mickey Mansfield

Children

Creatures that should be seen and not smelt.

Joyce Jillson

A species of being that, not having yet learnt how to be hypocritical, are quite frank about pointing out their own merits.

Virginia Graham

Items that have become so expensive, only the poor can afford them.

Hal Roach

A great comfort in your old age – and they help you reach it easier too.

Lionel Kauffmann

Chivalry

A man's inclination to protect a woman from every man but himself.

Brian Johnston

Chocolate

What, according to research, is liked by
fourteen out of every ten individuals.

Sandra Boynton

Chop

A piece of leather skilfully attached to a bone,
and then administered to patients at restaurants.

Ambrose Bierce

Christian

One who believes that the New Testament is a
divinely inspired book, admirably suited to the
spiritual needs of his neighbour.

Ambrose Bierce

A man who feels repentance on Sunday for
what he did on Saturday and is going to do
again on Monday.

Thomas Ybarra

Christianity

Possibly a good idea, if somebody tried it.

George Bernard Shaw

Christmas

That magical time of the year when all your
money disappears.

Hal Roach

The time of year when you put too many
pounds onto your body... and take too many
out of your bank account.

Mary Mannion

Chrysanthemum

A flower which, by any other name, would be
much easier to spell.

William Johnson

Church of England, The

The perfect church for those who don't go to
church.

Gerald Priestland

Chutzpah

When you murder both your parents, and then
throw yourself at the mercy of the courts
because you're an orphan.

Anon.

Cigarette

The perfect type of pleasure; it is exquisite and it also leaves one unsatisfied.

Oscar Wilde

Cinema

The most beautiful fraud in the world.

Jean-Luc Godard

Circulating Library

An evergreen tree of diabolical knowledge.

Richard Brinsley Sheridan

Circumlocution

A literary trick whereby the writer who has nothing to say breaks it gently to the reader.

Ambrose Bierce

City

A place where you're least likely to get a bite from a wild sheep.

Brendan Behan

Not a concrete jungle, but a human zoo.

Desmond Morris

Millions of people being lonely together.

Henry Thoreau

The only desert still available to us.

Albert Camus

Civil Servant

A person who doesn't make jokes.

Eugene Ionesco

Civil Service, The

A self-perpetuating oligarchy.

Lord Armstrong

Civilisation

A race between education and catastrophe.

H. G. Wells

The lamb's skin in which barbarism
masquerades.

T.B. Aldrich

A heap of rubble scavenged by scrawny
English Lit. vultures.

Malcolm Muggeridge

Barbarism made strong and luxurious by
mechanical power.

C.S. Lewis

Classic, A

Something that everybody wants to have read and nobody wants to read.

Mark Twain

Classical Music

What we keep hoping will turn into a tune.

Kin Hubbard

Classical Quotation

The parole of the literati.

Samuel Johnson

Cleanliness

What is almost as bad as godliness.

Samuel Butler

What is next to impossible.

Audrey Austin

Clergyman

A man who undertakes the management of our spiritual affairs as a method of bettering *his* temporal ones.

Ambrose Bierce

Clever Woman

One who knows how to give a man her own way.

Hal Roach

Clue

What the police find when they fail to find what they're looking for.

J.B. Morton

Cocaine

God's way of telling you you're making too much money.

Robin Williams

Cocktail Party

A device for paying off obligations to people you wouldn't want to invite to dinner.

Noel Coward

Bottom-sniffing raised to the point of formal ceremony.

Lawrence Durrell

Cocktails

Drinks which have all the disagreeability of a disinfectant, with none of the utility.

Shane Leslie

Coffee

What, in England, tastes like a chemical experiment.

Agatha Christie

Coffee Break

America's biggest advance yet in the area of communications.

Herbert Prochnow

Coin

Something that's useful for getting the wrong number in a telephone box.

Jack Cruise

Coitus

Like a slight attack of apoplexy.

Pauline Shapler

Collision

What happens when two motorists go after the same pedestrian.

Bob Newhart

Comedian

The goof that relays the olden gag.

Herbert Prochnow

Comedy

Emotional hang-gliding.

Robin Williams

Society protecting itself with a smile.

J.B. Priestley

A funny way of being serious.

Peter Ustinov

The last refuge of the non-conformist mind.

Gilbert Seldes

Like sodomy, an unnatural act.

Marty Feldman

Comics

Famously tragic people.

Marlon Brando

Commerce

A kind of transaction in which A plunders for B the goods of C, and for compensation B picks the pocket of D of money belonging to E.

Ambrose Bierce

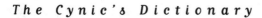

Commendation

The tribute we pay to achievements that
resemble, but do not equal, our own.

Ambrose Bierce

Committee

A *cul-de-sac* down which ideas are lured and
then quietly strangled.

John A. Lincoln

An animal with four back legs.

John Le Carré

A group of people who keep minutes and
waste hours.

Milton Berle

A small group of the unqualified, appointed
by the unthinking, to undertake the utterly
unnecessary.

Fibber Magee

Common Sense

The collection of prejudices acquired by the
age of eighteen.

Albert Einstein

Genius dressed up in working clothes.

Ralph Waldo Emerson

Communism

Socialism with electricity.

Vladimir Lenin

A bit like Prohibition – a good idea, but it won't work.

Will Rogers

Communist

A socialist without a sense of humour.

George Cutton

Compassion

The albatross of the liberal.

J.B. Priestley

Compliance

The path of least persistence.

Gordon Baker

Compromise

The art of dividing a cake in such a way that everyone believes he has the biggest piece.

Ludwig Erhard

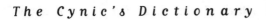

What used to mean half a loaf is better than no bread, but among modern statesmen it seems to mean half a loaf is better than the whole loaf.

G.K. Chesterton

Conceit

A polite form of self-imposed torture.

Henry Miller

God's gift to little men.

Bruce Barton

Concorde

A plane that gives you three extra hours to find your luggage.

Bob Hope

A plane that travels so fast, the air hostess slaps you on the face before you even tell her what you were thinking.

Bob Hope

Conclusion

What you reach when you get tired of thinking.

Martin Fischer

Conference

A gathering together of important people who singly can do nothing, but together decide that nothing can be done.

Fred Allen

Confession

The acknowledgement made to a priest of a sinful act committed by a friend, neighbour or acquaintance, and to which you reacted with righteous indignation.

Ambrose Bierce

Confidence

The feeling that makes one believe a man, even when one knows that one would lie in his place.

H.L. Mencken

Conflict

What begins at the moment of birth.

Jean Baker Miller

Connoisseur

Someone who can sip a glass of wine and tell you not only what year it was bottled, but who jumped on the grapes.

Stanley Davis

Conscience

What your mother told you before you were six years old.

Brock Chisholm

An anticipation of the opinions of others.

Henry Taylor

Ought-to suggestion.

H.L. Mencken

The thing that hurts when everything else feels good.

Herbert Prochnow

What makes cowards of us all.

William Shakespeare

What makes egotists of us all.

Oscar Wilde

The inner voice that warns us that someone may be looking.

H.L. Mencken

Something that doesn't only make cowards of us all, but dyspeptics too.

Helen Simpson

What makes a boy tell his mother before his sister does.

Franklin P. Jones

Conservative

A statesman who is enamoured of existing evils, as distinguished from a liberal, who wishes to replace them with others.

Ambrose Bierce

Someone who believes in reform, but not now.

Mort Sahl

Someone who demands a square deal for the rich.

David Frost

A liberal who got mugged the night before.

Frank Rizzo

Conservatism

The worship of dead revolutions.

Clinton Rossiter

Consistency

The last refuge of the unimaginative.

Oscar Wilde

Contraceptives

Items that should be used on every conceivable occasion.

Spike Milligan

Contract

An agreement that's binding only on the weaker party.

Frederick Sawyer

Conversation

The enemy of good wine and food.

Alfred Hitchcock

Convictions

More dangerous enemies of truth than lies.

Friedrich Nietzsche

Coquette

Like a recruiting sergeant, always on the look-out for fresh victims.

Douglas Jerrold

Correct English

The slang of the prigs who write history and essays.

George Eliot

Corruption

The most infallible symptom of constitutional liberty.

Edward Gibbon

Cosmos, The

The smallest hole that a man can hide his head in.

G.K. Chesterton

Country, The

A kind of healthy grave.

Sydney Smith

Court

An assemblage of noble and distinguished beggars.

Charles Talleyrand

The period of dating during which a girl decides whether she can do any better.

Herbert Prochnow

Courtroom

A place where Jesus Christ and Judas Iscariot would be equals, with the betting odds favouring Judas.

H.L. Mencken

Crank

A man with a new idea – until it succeeds.

Mark Twain

Crazy Pavement

A walking area that's not all it's cracked up
to be.

Anon.

Creator, The

A comedian whose audience is afraid to laugh.

H.L. Mencken

Credit

A system whereby a person who can't pay a
debt gets another person who can't pay it either
to say he can.

W.C. Fields

Cricket

A game invented by religious fundamentalists
to explain the idea of eternal hell to
non-Christian indigenous peoples of the
former British Empire.

Joe O'Connor

Crime

A logical extension of the sort of behaviour
that is often considered perfectly reasonable in
legitimate business.

Ambrose Bierce

Criminal

A person with predatory instincts who has not
sufficient capital to form a corporation.

Howard Scott

Critic

A gong at a railway crossing clanging loudly
and vainly as the train goes by.

Christopher Morley

A bunch of biases held loosely together by a
sense of taste.

Witney Balliett

A man who knows the way but can't drive
the car.

Kenneth Tynan

A eunuch in the harem.

Brendan Behan

A louse in the locks of literature.

Lord Tennyson

A failed writer – but then so are most writers!

T.S. Eliot

A newspaperman whose sweetheart ran away with an actor.

Walter Winchell

Crook

A businessman without a shop.

Brendan Behan

Crowd

A group of people that always bring a lump to my wallet.

Eli Wallach

Cult

Not enough people to make a minority.

Robert Altman

Culture

Anything men do – and monkeys don't.

Lord Raglan

Curiosity

Little more than another name for hope.

J.C. Hare

Custard

A detestable substance produced by a malevolent conspiracy of the hen, the cow and the cook.

Ambrose Bierce

Cynic

A sentimentalist afraid of himself.

Lambert Jeffries

A blackguard whose faulty vision sees things as they are, not as they ought to be.

Ambrose Bierce

Someone who found out there wasn't any Santa Claus when he was ten, and is still upset about it.

James Gould Cozzens

Cynicism

Intellectual dandyism.

George Meredith

The intellectual cripple's substitute for intelligence.

Russell Lynes

An unpleasant way of telling the truth.

Lillian Hellman

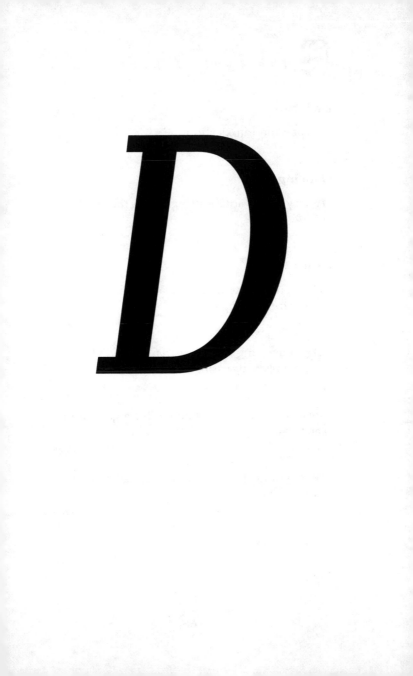

Dadaism

Turpentine intoxication.

Marcel Duchamp

Dancing

A very crude attempt to get into the rhythm of life.

George Bernard Shaw

Death

The penultimate commercial transaction finalised by Probate.

Bernard Rosenberg

The only thing society hasn't succeeded in completely vulgarising.

Aldous Huxley

Something that comes along like a gas bill one can't pay.

Anthony Burgess

What politically correct doctors call a Negative Patient Outcome.

John Koski

A slave's freedom.

Nikki Giovanni

Début

The first time a young girl is seen drunk in public.

F. Scott Fitzgerald

Decency

Indecency's conspiracy of silence.

F. Scott Fitzgerald

Decision

What a man makes when he can't get anyone to serve on a committee.

Fletcher Knebel

Décolletage

The only place men want depth in women.

Zsa Zsa Gabor

Deer-stalking

What would be a very fine sport if only the deer had a gun.

W.S. Gilbert

Delicatessen

A shop selling the worst parts of animals more expensively than the nice parts.

Mike Barfield

Demagogue

A person with whom we disagree as to which gang should mismanage the country.

Don Marquis

Democracy

A system in which you say what you like and do what you're told.

Gerard Barry

A system of choosing your dictators, after they've told you what you think it is you want to hear.

Alan Coren

Government by discussion – but it's only effective if you can stop people talking.

Clement Attlee

An institution in which the whole is equal to the scum of the parts.

Keith Preston

A political system that substitutes election by the incompetent many for appointment by the corrupt few.

George Bernard Shaw

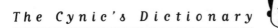
The aristocracy of blackguards.

Lord Byron

The worst form of government – except for all the others.

Winston Churchill

The art of running the circus from the monkey cage.

H.L. Mencken

The right to make the wrong choice.

Glenn Ford

The theory that holds that the common people know what they want, and deserve to get it good and hard.

H.L. Mencken

Despair

The price one pays for setting oneself an impossible dream.

Graham Greene

Detective Novel

The art for art's sake of yawning philistinism.

V.S. Pritchett

Devil, The

A gentleman who never goes where he's not welcome.

John A. Lincoln

Diagnosis

The physician's activity of determining the condition of the patient's purse in order to decide how sick to make him.

Ambrose Bierce

Dialect

Those terrible marks of the beast to the truly genteel.

Thomas Hardy

Dialogue

The bright things you would have liked to have said, except you didn't think of them in time.

Preston Sturges

Diamonds

The only type of ice that makes a woman feel warm.

Liz Taylor

Dictatorship

A country where they've taken the politics out of politics.

Mike Barfield

Something that's always in the future tense.

Sandra Bergeson

Dignity

The only thing you can't preserve in alcohol.

Edward Phillips

Dilettante

A person who goes to the theatre with a box of chocolates, a personally-autographed copy of the text... and two sleeping pills.

Anon.

Where wealth and literature meet.

Douglas Dunn

Diplomacy

The patriotic art of lying for one's country.

Ambrose Bierce

The art of saying 'Nice doggie' till you can find a rock.

Wynn Catlin

The art of letting someone else have your way.

David Frost

To do and say/ The nastiest thing in the nicest way.

Isaac Goldberg

The art of jumping into troubled waters without making a splash.

Art Linkletter

Diplomat

A man who always remembers a woman's birthday, but never her age.

Robert Frost

A person who thinks twice before saying nothing.

Fred Sawyer

A fellow that lets you do all the talking while he gets what he wants.

Kin Hubbard

Someone who tells you to go to hell in such a way that you think you'd enjoy the trip.

Caskie Stinnet

Disc Jockeys

Electronic lice.

Anthony Burgess

Discretion

Not the better part of biography.

Michael Holroyd

The polite word for hypocrisy.

Christine Keeler

Disillusionment

What takes place when a youngster asks his dad for help with his algebra.

Herbert Prochnow

Divorce

America's great contribution to marriage.

Edward Fawcett

Estranged bedfellows.

Mort Sahl

When a husband doesn't bring home the bacon anymore, but *mails* it.

Morty Craft

Fission after fusion.

Rita Mae Brown

The sacrament of adultery.

French proverb

Doctors

Men who prescribe medicines of which they
know little, to cure diseases of which
they know less, in human beings of whom
they know nothing.

Voltaire

Doctrine

Nothing but the skin of truth set up and
stuffed.

H. W. Beecher

Doctoral Thesis

The transference of bones from one graveyard
to another.

Frank Dobie

Dogmatism

Puppyism come to its full growth.

Douglas Jerrold

Dogs

Subsidiary deities designed to catch the over-
flow of the world's worship.

Ambrose Bierce

Dolphins

Animals that are so intelligent that, within a
few weeks of captivity, they can train a man to
stand on the edge of their pool and throw them
food three times a day.

Hal Roach

Donsmanship

The art of criticising without actually listening.

Stephen Potter

Door

What a dog is perpetually on the wrong
side of.

Ogden Nash

Draft, The

White people sending black people to fight
yellow people to protect the country they stole
from red people.

James Rado

Drama Critic

A person who surprises the playwright by informing him what he really meant.

Wilson Mizner

A man who leaves no turn unstoned.

George Bernard Shaw

Drama Criticism

An attempt to tattoo soap bubbles.

John Mason Brown

Drawing

The art of taking a line for a walk.

Paul Klee

Driving

America's last surviving form of guerrilla warfare.

Gene Perret

Drug

A substance which, if injected into a guinea pig, produces a scientific paper.

Paul Williams

Drugs

A spiritual form of gambling.

Norman Mailer

Drunk

An alcoholic who doesn't have to go to all those boring old meetings.

Jackie Gleason

Drunkenness

A condition that doesn't so much create a ' ' as bring it into view.

Seneca

Voluntary madness.

Seneca

Temporary suicide.

Bertrand Russell

A device people employ to avoid having to think of having anything to say.

Alan Simpson

Dublin

A place that's much worse than London, but not so bad as Iceland.

Samuel Johnson

A city with the great advantage that it's easy to get out of.

Oliver St John Gogarty

Dutch

Not so much a language as a disease of the throat.

Mark Twain

Duty

What largely consists of pretending the trivial is critical.

John Fowles

Dying

A very dull, dreary affair. My advice to you is to have nothing whatever to do with it.

Somerset Maugham

One of the few things that can be done just as easily lying down.

Woody Allen

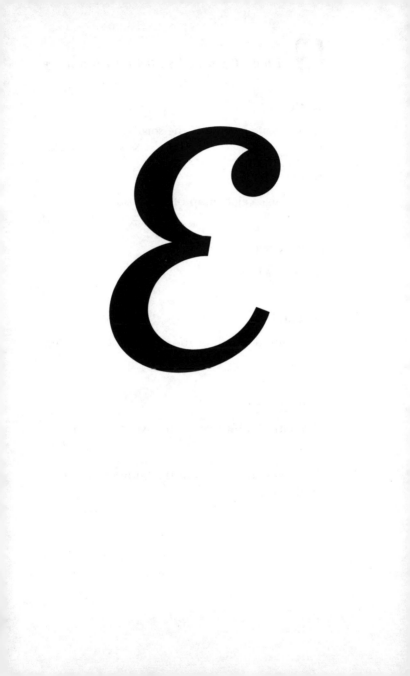

Earth

The lunatic asylum of the solar system.

Samuel Parkes Cadman

Easter

A national celebration of chocolate.

Mike Barfield

Easy Street

A blind alley.

Wilson Mizner

Eccentric

A person too rich or too powerful to be called crazy.

Eve Pollard

Ecology

A political substitute for the word 'mother'.

Jesse Unruh

The belief that a bird in the bush is worth two in the hand.

Stanley Gibbons

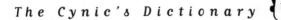

Economics

The one profession where you can gain great eminence without ever being right.

George Meany

Economists

Experts who will know tomorrow why the things they predicted yesterday didn't happen today.

Laurence Peter

People who spend their time re-arranging the deck chairs on the *Titanic*.

Ernest Schumacher

Those who cut down on other people's wages.

J.B. Morton

Economy

Going without something you want in case you should one day want something else you probably won't.

Anthony Hope

Purchasing the barrel of whiskey that you do not need for the price of the cow that you cannot afford.

Ambrose Bierce

Ecstasy

A drug so strong it makes white people think they can dance.

Lenny Henry

Edinburgh

A dignified spinster with syphilis.

Charles Higham

Editor

A man who takes a French poodle and clips him into the shape of a lion.

Emery Kelen

A person who separates the wheat from the chaff, and prints the chaff.

Adlai Stevenson

Edmonton

Not exactly the end of the world...but you can see it from there.

Ralph Klein

Education

The inculcation of the incomprehensible into the ignorant by the incompetent.

Josiah Stamp

What remains after we have forgotten
everything we've been taught.

George Savile

Something that demonstrates to you how little
other people know.

T.C. Haliburton

A method whereby one acquires a higher grade
of prejudices.

Laurence Peter

Learning what you didn't even know you didn't
know.

Daniel Boorstin

Egotism

A case of mistaken nonentity.

Barbara Stanwyck

An anaesthetic that dulls the pain of mediocrity.

Frank Leahy

Egotist

A person of low taste, more interested in
himself than in me.

Ambrose Bierce

Somebody whose best quality is the fact that he dosen't talk about others.

Lucille Harper

A person who likes mirrors, but can't understand why others do.

Peter Eldin

Eighth Commandment, The

One that wasn't made for bards.

Samuel Taylor Coleridge

Election

When the air is full of speeches...and vice versa.

Peter Eldin

Elephant

A mouse drawn to Government specifications.

John D. Sheridan

Elevator Operator

Someone who never hears the end of a good story.

Les Dawson

Elitist

Someone who corrects your spelling.

Mitchell Symons

Eloquence

The ability to describe Kim Basinger without using one's hands.

Michael Harkness

Employment

Death without the dignity.

Brendan Behan

Encourage

To confirm a fool in a folly that is beginning to hurt him.

Ambrose Bierce

Enema

An object used to brainwash men.

Nancy Grey

Enemy

A friend you got wise to.

Gene Perret

England

The heart of a rabbit in the body of a lion; the jaws of a serpent in the abode of popinjays.

Eugene Deschamps

The paradise of little men, and the purgatory of great ones.

Cardinal John Newman

A country infested with people who love to tell us what to do, but who very rarely seem to know what's going on.

Colin MacInnes

English

The perfect language to sell pigs in.

Michael Hartnett

A word in the dictionary between enema and entrails.

Tony Hancock

English, The

A race of cold-blooded queers with nasty complexions and terrible teeth who once conquered half the world, but still haven't figured out central heating.

P.J. O'Rourke

People who instantly admire any man who has
no talent and is modest about it.

James Agee

Those who never forgive a man for being
clever.

Lord Hailsham

Englishman

Somebody who is unable to like anyone who
cannot knock him down.

E.M. Forster

Someone who, even if he's alone, forms an
orderly queue of one.

George Mikes

Someone with all the qualities of a poker,
except its occasional warmth.

Daniel O'Connell

A creature who thinks he's being virtuous
when he's merely being uncomfortable.

George Bernard Shaw

Someone who never enjoys himself except for
a noble purpose.

A.P. Herbert

Envy

The basis of democracy.

Bertrand Russell

Epic

The easiest type of picture to make badly.

Charlton Heston

Any film with Charlton Heston in it.

James Agate

Epigram

A wisecrack that's played Carnegie Hall.

Oscar Levant

A platitude on its night out.

Philip Guedalla

Erudition

Dust shaken out of a book into an empty skull.

Ambrose Bierce

A charming thing when held firmly in leash,
but not so attractive when turned
loose upon a defenceless, unerudite public.

Agnes Repplier

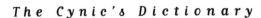
ESP

Essentially Silly People.

Cleveland Amory

Esprit de Corps

That typically English characteristic for which there is no English translation.

Frank Adcock

'Et Cetera'

The expression that makes people think you known more than you do.

Herbert Prochnow

Eternity

Paying for a car on the instalment plan.

Jack Benny

Ethics

A Christian holding four aces.

Mark Twain

What stays in the Preface of the average business science book.

Peter Drucker

Etiquette

The art of making company feel at home...when you wish they were.

Henny Youngman

Eulogy

Praise of a person who has either wealth or power, or the consideration to be dead.

Ambrose Bierce

Eunuch

A man who has had his works cut out for him.

Robert Byrne

Exaggeration

The cheapest form of humour.

Elizabeth Peters

A truth that has lost its temper.

Kahlil Gibran

Excellence

What makes people nervous.

Shana Alexander

Executive

An ulcer with authority.

Fred Allen

Executive Ability

Getting someone else to do the work.

J. G. Pollock

Exhibitionist

The kind of guy who, when he opens the fridge door and the light comes on, he does twenty minutes.

Jerry Lewis

Existence

Just a brief crack of light between two eternities of darkness.

Vladimir Nabokov

Existentialism

A philosophy with no future.

Audrey Austin

Existentialist

Someone who swims with the tide – but faster.

Quentin Crisp

Experience

The name everyone gives to their mistakes.

Oscar Wilde

What you get when you're looking for something else.

Mary Pettibone Poole

A good teacher – but she sends in terrific bills.

Minna Antrim

Expert

A man who has stopped thinking.

Frank Lloyd Wright

Someone who has made all the mistakes that can be made, but in a very narrow field.

Niels Bohr

A person who can take something you knew already and make it sound confusing.

Herbert Prochnow

Extravagance

The way the other fellow spends his money.

Harry Thompson

Anything you buy that is of no earthly use to your wife.

Franklin Adams

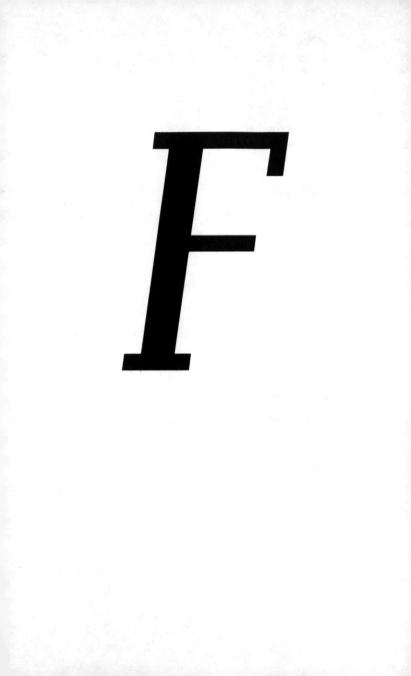

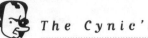

Face

A carving abandoned as altogether too unpromising for completion.

H.G. Wells

Failure

Anyone seen on a bus after the age of thirty.

Nicholas Ray

Faith

Not wanting to know what is true.

Friedrich Nietzsche

An illogical belief in the occurrence of the improbable.

H.L. Mencken

Falklands War

Two bald men arguing over a comb.

Jorge Luis Borges

Fame

Being asked to sign your autograph on the back of a cigarette packet.

Billy Connolly

Failure disguised as money.

Brendan Behan

Being pecked to death by a thousand pigeons.
Bob Hoskins

The perfume of heroic deeds.
Socrates

An empty bubble.
James Grainger

A comic distinction shared with Roy Rogers' horse and Miss Watermelon of 1955.
Flannery O'Connor

Familiarity

What breeds content – and children.
Mark Twain

Family

A bowling alley inside your head.
Martin Mull

Family Man

Someone who has replaced the money in his wallet with pictures of his wife and kids.
Leopold Fechtner

Famous

Conspicuously miserable.
Ambrose Bierce

Fanatic

A man who does what he thinks the Lord
would do if He knew the facts of the case.

Finley Peter Dunne

One who sticks to his guns, whether they're
loaded or not.

Franklin P. Jones

Fanaticism

Re-doubling your effort when you've forgotten
your aim.

George Santayana

Farce

A genre that's nearer to tragedy in its essence
than comedy is.

Samuel Taylor Coleridge

Tragedy with the trousers down.

Brian Rix

Farm

An irregular patch of nettles containing a fool
and his wife, who didn't know enough to stay
in the city.

S.J. Perelman

Capitalism plus murder.

Upton Sinclair

A counter-revolution against a revolution that never took place.

Ignazio Silone

Fascist

Anyone who disagrees with you.

John Koski

Fashion

A form of ugliness so intolerable, we have to alter it every six months.

Oscar Wilde

What is made to become unfashionable.

Coco Chanel

What we have instead of God.

Malcolm Bradbury

Fashions

Induced epidemics.

George Bernard Shaw

Faults

What people discover they have after they get married.

Milton Berle

Federal Aid

A system of making the money that was taken away from the people look like a gift when handed back.

Carl Workman

Feminist

A woman, usually ill-favoured, in whom the film-making instinct has replaced the maternal one.

Barry Humphries

Fiddle

An instrument to tickle human ears by function of a horse's tail on the entrails of a cat.

Ambrose Bierce

Fidelity

A virtue peculiar to those who are about to be betrayed.

Ambrose Bierce

Putting all your eggs in one bastard.

Dorothy Parker

Fifties, The

The decade when air was clean and sex dirty.

George Burns

Ten years of foreplay.

Germaine Greer

Fifty

The age at which actions creak louder than words.

Anon.

Fighting

Like champagne, what goes to the heads of cowards as quickly as of heroes.

Margaret Mitchell

Filing Cabinet

A useful container for losing things alphabetically.

Kevin Goldstein-Jackson

Film

A petrified fountain of thought.

Jean Cocteau

The world in an hour and a half.

Jean-Luc Godard

Film Director

A ringmaster, psychiatrist and referee.

Robert Aldrich

A policeman, a midwife, a psychoanalyst, a sycophant...and a bastard.

Billy Wilder

Films

What have given me an opportunity to do things that normally you'd be locked up and executed for.

Lee Marvin

Fin de Siècle

The tail light of a bicycle.

Russell Lucas

Financier

A pawnbroker with imagination.

A. W. Pinero

Finnegans Wake

One long spelling mistake.

Ernest Cox

First Love

A little love, and a lot of curiosity.

George Bernard Shaw

Fishing

The activity of doing something when you're not doing anything.

Mort Sahl

An excuse to drink in the daytime.

Jimmy Cannon

Fishing Rod

A stick with a worm at one end and a fool at the other.

Samuel Johnson

Flatterer

Someone who says things to your face that he wouldn't dare say behind your back.

George Millington

Flattery

A bit like a cigarette – all right as long as you don't inhale.

Adlai Stevenson

A false coin that is only current thanks to our vanity.

Duc de la Rochefoucauld

Flirtation

An expression of considered desire coupled with an admission of its impracticality.

Marya Mannes

Attention without intention.

Max O'Rell

Flirts

Women whose favourite man is…the next one.

Justin Peters

Floor

The only thing that can stop hair falling.

Will Rogers

Florida

God's waiting room.

Glenn le Grice

Food

The most important part of a balanced diet.

Fran Lebowitz

Fools

Ninety-nine percent of the people in the world – and the rest of us are in great danger of contagion.

William Whyte

People who are in a terrible, overwhelming majority, all the wide world over.

Henrik Ibsen

Football

Not a matter of life and death – it's much more important than that.

Bill Shankly

A contact sport - just like Christmas shopping.

Gene Perret

A game designed to keep coal-miners off the streets.

Jimmy Breslin

All very well as a game for rough girls, but it is hardly suitable for delicate boys.

Oscar Wilde

Footballers

Miry gladiators whose sole purpose in life is to position a surrogate human head between two poles.

Elizabeth Hogg

Foresight

Spending 50 years of adult life in comparative drudgery in order to be able to spend the remaining ten in a nursing home.

Lambert Jeffries

Forgetfulness

The true token of greatness.

Elbert Hubbard

A gift of God bestowed upon debtors in compensation for their destitution of conscience.

Ambrose Bierce

Forgiveness

A stratagem to throw an offender off his guard and catch him red-handed in his next offence.

Ambrose Bierce

Fox

A wolf who sends flowers.

Ruth Weston

France

The largest country in Europe, which is a great boon for drunkards, who need room to fall.

Alan Coren

A country where the money falls apart in your hands and you can't tear the toilet paper.

Billy Wilder

The only country in the world where the rich are sometimes brilliant.

Lillian Hellman

Free Verse

Like free love – a contradiction in terms.

G.K. Chesterton

Freedom

Another word for nothing left to lose.

Kris Kristofferson

Friend

Someone who sticks by you even when he gets to know you real well.

E.C. McKenzie

Friends

Not necessarily the people you like best; merely those you met first.

Peter Ustinov

People who tell you all the nice things you already knew about yourself.

Anon.

God's apology for relations.

Hugh Kingsmill

Thermometers by which we judge the temperature of our fortune.

Countess of Blessington

Friendship

A relationship by which we undertake to exchange small favours for big ones.

Baron de Montesquieu

A holy passion, so sweet and steady and loyal and enduring in its nature that it will last through a whole lifetime – if either party isn't asked to lend money.

Mark Twain

Love without his wings.

Lord Byron

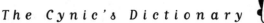

Fun

A bit like life insurance: the older you get, the more it costs.

Kin Hubbard

Funeral

A pageant where we show our respect for the dead by enriching the undertaker.

Ambrose Bierce

Interruptions of traffic.

George Ade

Funferalls.

James Joyce

Fussiness

Being in the company of several other old ladies of both sexes.

Charles Dickens

Future, The

The most expensive luxury in the world.

Thornton Wilder

Not what it used to be.

Paul Valery

Something which everyone reaches at the rate
of 60 miles an hour whatever he does, whoever
he is.

C.S. Lewis

The only kind of property masters willingly
concede to slaves.

Albert Camus

The period of time in which our affairs
prosper, our friends are true, and our happiness
assured.

Ambrose Bierce

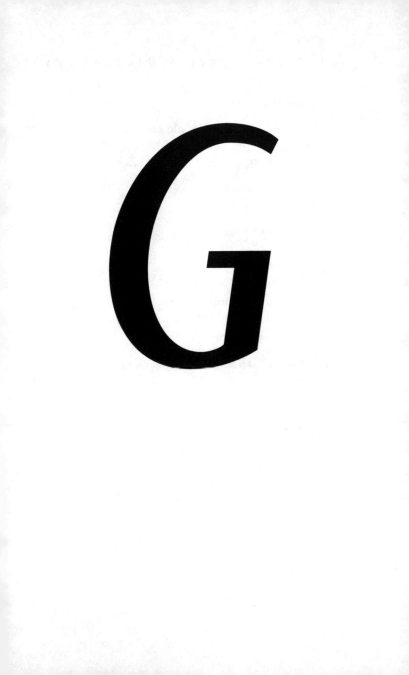

Gambling

A process whereby people take your money and then tell you what a good time you're having.

Anon.

Garden

A thing of beauty and a job for ever.

Barry Tobin

Genealogy

An account of one's descent from a man who didn't particularly care to trace his own.

Ambrose Bierce

Tracing yourself back to people better than you are.

John Garland Pollard

Genius

Anyone under ten years of age.

Fidelma Connell

A man who can re-wrap a new shirt and not have any pins left over.

Dino Levi

The capacity for evading hard work.

Elbert Hubbard

One per cent inspiration and 99 per cent perspiration.

Thomas Edison

An African who dreams up snow.

Vladimir Nabokov

Genius Worship

The inevitable sign of an uncreative age.

Clive Bell

Gentility

What's left over from rich ancestors after the money is gone.

John Ciardi

Gentleman

Someone who gets out of the bath to go to the toilet.

Freddie Trueman

One who never heard a story before.

Austin O' Malley

One who never strikes a woman without provocation.

H.L. Mencken

A patient wolf.

Henrietta Tiarks

Somebody who need not necessarily *know* Latin, but he should at least have forgotten it.

Brander Matthews

Gentleman Farmer

A man who raises nothing but his hat.

Don Bale

German

A language which was devised solely to afford the speaker the opportunity to spit at strangers under the guise of polite conversation.

Anon.

Gesticulation

Any movement made by a foreigner.

J.B. Morton

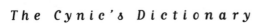

Gift Shop

A place where you can see all the things you hope your friends won't send you for Christmas.

Jack Wolsey

Gigolo

A fee-male.

Isaac Goldberg

Glamour

Standing still and looking stupid.

Hedy Lamarr

Glutton

A person who takes the piece of pastry you wanted.

Anon.

Gluttony

Not a secret vice.

Orson Welles

A sign that something is eating us.

Peter de Vries

Goats

Sheep from broken homes, according to liberals.

Malcolm Bradbury

God

That dumping ground of our dreams.

Jean Rostand

Operationally, somebody who's beginning to resemble not a ruler, but the last fading smile of a cosmic Cheshire cat.

Sir Julian Huxley

Somebody who doesn't belong to any religion.

Michael Caine

Gold-digger

A woman who spells matrimony 'matter o' money'.

Louis Safian

Gold Rush

What happens when a line of chorus girls spot a man with a bank roll.

Mae West

Golf

An ineffectual attempt to direct an uncontrollable sphere into an inaccessible hole with instruments ill-adapted for the purpose.

Winston Churchill

The most popular method of beating round the bush.

Leopold Fechtner

Cow pasture pool.

O.K. Bovard

An expensive way of playing marbles.

G.K. Chesterton

A game to be played between cricket and death.

Colin Ingleby-McKenzie

Good Behaviour

The last refuge of mediocrity.

Henry S. Haskins

Good Fences

What make good neighbours.

Robert Frost

Good Film

When the price of the dinner, the theatre admission and the babysitter were worth it.

Alfred Hitchcock

Good Listener

A good talker with a sore throat.

Katharine Whitehorn

Good Politician

A breed quite as unthinkable as an honest burglar.

H.L. Mencken

Good Reviews

Merely stays of execution.

Dustin Hoffman

Good Taste

The worst vice ever invented.

Edith Sitwell

Good-Time Girl

Someone who, when confronted with two indulgences, chooses the one she hasn't tried before.

Mae West

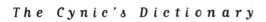

Gossip

The art of saying nothing in a way that leaves practically nothing left unsaid.

Walter Winchell

When you hear something you like about someone you don't.

Earl Wilson

Vice enjoyed vicariously.

Elbert Hubbard

The art form of the man and woman in the street.

W.H. Auden

The only industry that finances its own blackmail.

Walter Wanger

A sort of smoke that comes from the dirty tobacco-pipes of those who diffuse it.

George Eliot

News running ahead of itself in a red satin dress.

Liz Smith

The Cynic's Dictionary

Gourmet

A glutton with brains.

Philip J. Haberman

Government

The only known vessel that leaks from the top.

James Reston

The only organisation that operates on a deficit and still makes money.

Vern McLellan

A necessary evil in its best state; in its worst – an intolerable one.

Thomas Paine

Government Bureau

The nearest thing to eternal life that we'll see on this earth.

Ronald Reagan

Governments

Structures that will last as long as the under-taxed can defend themselves against the over-taxed.

Bernard Berenson

Grammar

The grave of letters.

Elbert Hubbard

Grand Old Man

A North American with snow-white hair who has managed to stay out of jail till 80.

Stephen Leacock

Gratitude

A sickness suffered by dogs.

Joseph Stalin

Grave

A place where the dead are laid to await the coming of the medical student.

Ambrose Bierce

Growing Old

Like being increasingly penalised for a crime you haven't committed.

Anthony Powell

Guests

People who, like fish, smell after three days.

Anon.

Guilty Conscience

The mother of invention.

Carolyn Wells

Gynaecologist

A mechanic who never owned a car.

Carrie Snow

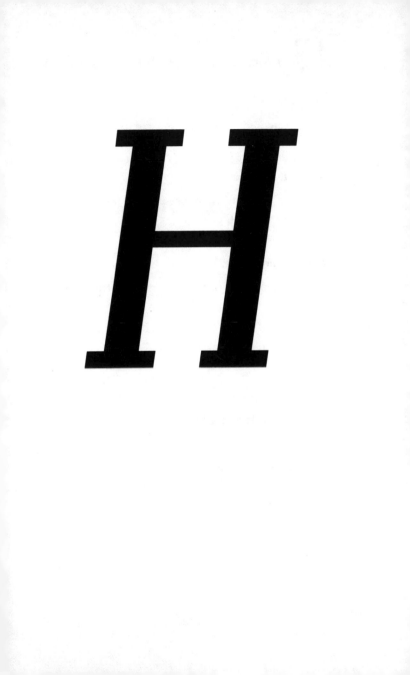

Habit

The ballast that chains a dog to his vomit.

Samuel Beckett

Hamlet

A great play, but there are far too many quotations in it.

Hugh Leonard

Hangover

When the brew of the night meets the dark of the day.

Brendan Behan

The wrath of grapes.

Jeffrey Barnard

Happiness

Good health and a bad memory.

Ingrid Bergman

A man with a wife to tell him what to do – and a secretary to do it.

Lord Mancroft

Not so much having what you want, as wanting what you have.

Hyman Schachtel

Knowing that you don't require happiness.

William Saroyan

Watching TV at your girlfriend's house during a power failure.

Bob Hope

Getting a bill you've already paid, so you can sit down and write a really nasty letter.

Peter Nero

A warm bedpan.

Christopher Hudson

An interval between periods of unhappiness.

Don Marquis

An agreeable sensation arising from contemplating the misery of another.

Ambrose Bierce

Harlot

The good time that's been had by all.

Bette Davis

Harpsichord

An instrument whose sound resembles that of a bird cage played with toasting forks.

Sir Thomas Beecham

Hatred

The coward's revenge for being intimidated.

George Bernard Shaw

Health Addict

A person who eats health food so he won't ruin his health and have to eat health food.

Leopold Fechtner

Heathen

A benighted creature who has the folly to worship something he can see and feel.

Ambrose Bierce

Heaven

The Coney Island of the Christian imagination.

Elbert Hubbard

The ultimate retirement village.

Gene Perret

A place which, as conventionally conceived, is so dull, so useless, so miserable, that nobody has ever ventured to describe a whole day in it – though plenty of people have described a day at the seaside.

George Bernard Shaw

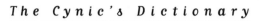

An English policeman, a French cook, a German engineer, an Italian lover - and everything organised by the Swiss.

John Elliott

Hell

An English cook, a French engineer, a German policeman, a Swiss lover - and everything organised by the Italians.

John Elliott

Other people.

Jean-Paul Sartre

Hen

Only an egg's way of making another egg.

Samuel Butler

Heredity

What a man believes in until his son begins to behave like a delinquent.

Mort Sahl

The principle which dictates that, if your parents didn't have any progeny, the likelihood is that you won't either.

Jon Froy

Heresy

Nothing but the bridge between two orthodoxies.

Francis Hackett

Heretic

Original thinker.

Ben Elton

Hermaphroditism

An end in itself.

Anon.

Heroism

The shortest-lived profession on earth.

Will Rogers

Highbrow

Someone who talks fluently about something neither of you understand, and makes you feel it's your fault.

Milton Berle

A man who can listen to the William Tell overture without thinking of Robin Hood.

Niall Toibin

Hip

The sophistication of the wise primitive in a giant jungle.

Norman Mailer

Historian

A prophet in reverse.

Friedrich von Schegel

Historians

Unsuccessful novelists.

H.L. Mencken

History

A nightmare from which I'm trying to awake.

James Joyce

An account, mostly false, of events, mostly unimportant, which were brought about by rulers, mostly knaves, and soldiers, mostly fools.

Ambrose Bierce

The sum total of the things that could have been avoided.

Konrad Adenauer

A fable agreed upon.

Napoleon

More or less bunk.

Henry Ford

Hobbies

Abominations, like all consuming interests
and passions that do not lead directly to large,
personal gain.

Fran Lebowitz

Holiday

Time off given to employees to remind them
that the company they work for can get along
fine without them.

Louise Norris

What makes you feel good enough to go back
to work, and poor enough so that you *have* to.

Revd James Simpson

Holidays

Things people who are bored with their jobs
take.

Madonna

Holiday Resort

A place where they charge you enough for the
eleven months you're not there.

Herbert Prochnow

Holland

Such a low country, it's only saved by being dammed.

Thomas Hood

Hollywood

A sewer with service from the Ritz Carlton.

Wilson Mizner

A place where they only know a single word of more than one syllable – fillum.

Louis Sherwin

An asylum run by the inmates.

Laurence Stallings

Where people from Iowa mistake each other for movie stars.

Fred Allen

Hollywood Aristocrats

People who can trace their ancestry all the way back to their parents.

Anon.

Hollywood Money

Like congealed snow: it melts in your hands.

Dorothy Parker

Home

The place where, when you have to go there, they have to take you in.

Robert Frost

The girl's prison and the woman's workhouse.

George Bernard Shaw

A place where part of the family waits till the rest of the family brings the car back.

Earl Wilson

Honest Politician

Someone who, when he is bought, will stay bought.

Simon Cameron

Honesty

The best policy – unless you happen to be an exceptionally good liar.

Jerome K. Jerome

Hope

The universal liar.

R. G. Ingersoll

Disappointment deferred.

Burton Baldry

Horse

An animal that's dangerous at both ends, and severely uncomfortable in the middle.

Ian Fleming

Horse Sense

The instinct that keeps horses from betting on humans.

Josephine Tey

Hospital

A building that ought to have the recovery room adjoining the cashier's office.

Francis Walsh

Hospitality

The virtue which induces us to feed and lodge certain persons who are not in need of food and lodging.

Ambrose Bierce

House

A machine for living in.

Le Corbusier

House of Lords, The

A model for how to care for the elderly.

Frank Field

Good evidence of life after death.

Lord Soper

The British Outer Mongolia for retired politicians.

Tony Benn

Housework

Something you do that nobody notices until you don't do it.

Mary Mannion

Human Being

An ingenious assembly of portable plumbing.

Robert Morley

Humanism

Progressivist optimism modified by fashionable despair.

Bernard Williams

Humour

Despair refusing to take itself seriously.

Arland Ussher

The first of the gifts to perish in a foreign tongue.

Virginia Woolf

Humiliation

Being given a bedpan by a stranger who calls you by your first name.

Maggie Kuhn

Hunting

The most effective way of getting rid of vermin - providing a sufficient number of them fall off their horses and break their necks.

Hugh Leonard

Ninety per cent of the fun of war for 10 per cent of the risk.

Philip Warburton Lee

Husband

Somebody who's chiefly a good lover when he's betraying his wife.

Marilyn Monroe

A man who uses both hands to drive the car.

Leopold Fechtner

The Cynic's Dictionary

Husbands

Like fires – they go out when unattended.

Zsa Zsa Gabor

Hygiene

The corruption of medicine by morality.

H.L. Mencken

Hypocrisy

The homage paid by vice to virtue.

Duc de La Rochefoucauld

Prejudice with a halo.

Ambrose Bierce

Hypocrite

A person who sows his wild oats from Monday to Friday, and then goes to Mass on Sunday to pray for a crop failure.

Liam Clancy

Hysteria

A snake whose scales are tiny mirrors in which the dead world takes on a semblance of life.

Nathaniel West

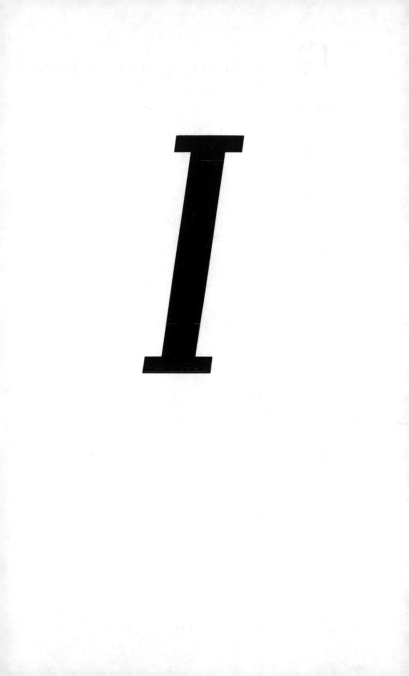

Idealism

The noble toga that political gentlemen drape over their will to power.

Aldous Huxley

Idealist

One who, on noticing that a rose smells better than a cabbage, concludes that it will also make better soup.

H.L. Mencken

Idlers

People who rust on their laurels.

Louis Safian

Idling

Something one can enjoy when one has plenty of work to do.

Jerome K. Jerome

Ignorance

Like a delicate, exotic fruit; touch it, and the bloom is gone.

Oscar Wilde

Immigration

The sincerest form of flattery.

Denis Norden

Immortality

An over-rated commodity.

S.N. Behrman

A fate worse than death.

Edgar Shoaff

What is longed for by those who would not
know what to do with themselves on a rainy
Sunday afternoon.

Susan Ertz

Impatience

Waiting in a hurry.

Sarah Pollard

Impiety

Your irreverence towards my deity.

Ambrose Bierce

The soul of wit.

Somerset Maugham

'In Conclusion'

The phrase that wakes up the audience.

Herbert Prochnow

Incest

Sibling ribaldry.

John Crosbie

Incinerator

A writer's best friend.

Thornton Wilder

Income

What you can't live without – or within.

Vern McLellan

Income Tax

The hardest thing in the world to understand.

Albert Einstein

Income Tax Returns

The most imaginative fiction being written today.

Herman Wouk

Inconvenience

Death, taxes and childbirth!

Margaret Mitchell

Inexperience

What makes a young man do what an older man says is impossible.

Herbert Prochnow

Inflation

Prosperity with high blood pressure.

Arnold Glasgow

The only form of taxation that can be imposed without legislation.

Milton Friedman

When half your money goes up in smoke, and you need the other half to put out the fire.

Leopold Fechtner

When you're wealthy and you can no longer afford the things you bought when you were poor.

Robert Orben

When prices go from reasonable to expensive to 'How much have you got with you?'

Bob Hope

Initiative

Successful disobedience.

John Fenton

Ink

A villainous compound of taumogallate of iron, gum-arabic and water, chiefly used to facilitate the inflection of idiocy and promote intellectual crime.

Ambrose Bierce

Insanity

The logic of an accurate mind overtaxed.

Oliver Wendell Holmes Jnr.

To art what garlic is to salad.

Augustus Saint-Gaudens

A hereditary condition – you get it from your children.

Sam Levenson

A perfectly rational adjustment to an insane world.

R.D. Laing

Insight

The titillating knack of hurting.

Colette

Inspiration

Inhaling the memory of an act never experienced.

Ned Rorem

Insurance

A guarantee that no matter how many necessities a person has to forego all through life, death is something to which he can still look forward.

Fred Allen

An ingenious modern game of chance in which the player is permitted to enjoy the comfortable conviction that he is beating the man who keeps the table.

Ambrose Bierce

Intellectual

A man who takes more words than necessary to tell more than he knows.

Dwight Eisenhower

A man who doesn't know how to park a bike.

Spiro Agnew

One who can think without moving his lips.

Anon.

Intercourse

The pure, sterile, formal expression of man's contempt for women.

Andrea Dworkin

Interpretation

Revenge of the intellect upon art.

Susan Sontag

Interpreter

One who enables two people of different languages to understand each other by repeating to each what it would have been to the interpreter's advantage for the the other to have said.

Ambrose Bierce

Intolerance

Being intolerant of the intolerant.

George Eliot

Invention

The mother of necessity.

Thornton Veblen

Ireland

A country full of genius, but with absolutely no talent.

Hugh Leonard

The sow that eats her farrow.

James Joyce

The only place in the world where procrastination takes on a sense of urgency.

Dave Allen

The only country in the world where you can get drunk and not wake up the next morning with a guilty conscience.

John Huston

Irish, The

A race of people who don't know what they want and are prepared to fight to the death to get it.

Sidney Littlewood

A fair people – they never speak well of each other.

Samuel Johnson

Irish Literary Movement

Two writers on speaking terms with one another.

Hugh Leonard

Islamic Moderate

One who believes that the firing squad should be democratically elected.

Henry Kissinger

Israel

The only country where one can say of someone that he is a Jew without being an anti-semite.

Jean-Paul Sartre

Italy

A country so blessed, that for every weed they destroy, two spring up in its place.

Leonardo Sciascia

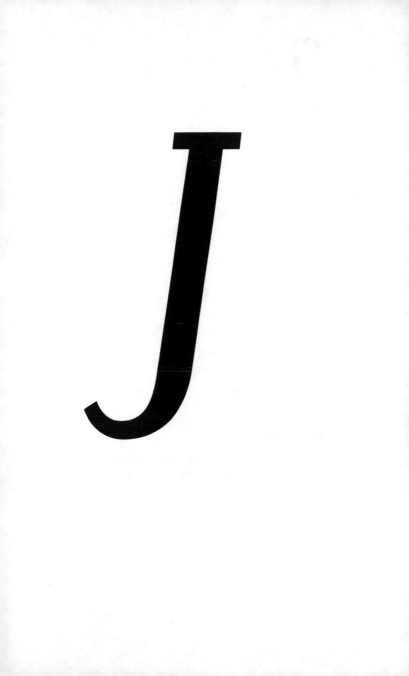

Jazz

Music invented by demons for the torture of imbeciles.

Henry Van Dyke

Jealousy

The dragon which slays love under the pretence of keeping it alive.

Havelock Ellis

Jet Travel

What lets us see less and less of more and more faster and faster.

Leopold Fechtner

Jews

A race of people like anyone else, only more so.

Arnold Foster

Journalism

A profession whose business it is to explain to others what it personally doesn't understand.

Lord Northcliffe

Organised gossip.

Edward Eggleston

Survival of the vulgarest.

Oscar Wilde

A walk of life that consists of saying
'Lord Jones is dead' to people who didn't
know he was alive.

G.K. Chesterton

The ability to meet the challenge of filling
space.

Rebecca West

The only thinkable alternative to working.

Jeffrey Barnard

The last refuge of the literary mediocre.

Brendan Behan

Journalist

A man who lies in the sun all day, then goes
home to his typewriter to lie some more.

Frank Sinatra

Judge

A law student who marks his own examination
papers.

H.L. Mencken

Judgement Day

God's audit.

Hal Roach

Jury

A body of twelve men and women selected to decide which of the contestants has the better lawyer.

E.C. Foster

A group of twelve men who, having lied to the judge about their hearing, health and business engagements, have failed to fool him.

H.L. Mencken

A group of twelve people of average ignorance.

Herbert Spencer

Juvenile Delinquents

People who have been given a free hand – but not in the proper place.

Hal Roach

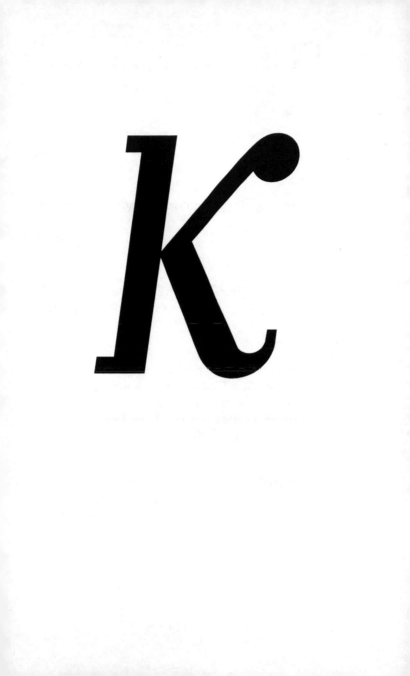

Killing

The ultimate simplification of life.

Hugh MacDiarmid

Kilt

An unrivalled garment for fornication...and diarrhoea.

John Masters

Kiss

A comma, a question mark or an exclamation point – basic grammar every woman ought to know.

Mistinguett

What originated when the first male reptile licked the first female reptile, implying in a subtle, complicated way that she was as succulent as the small reptile he had had for dinner the night before.

F. Scott Fitzgerald

Application on the top floor for a job in the basement.

Brian Johnston

Kitchenette

A narrow aisle that runs between a gas stove and a can of tomatoes.

Bob Burns

Kleptomaniac

A person who helps himself because he can't help himself.

Henry Morgan

Knowledge

Power...if you know it about the right person.

Ethel Watts Mumford

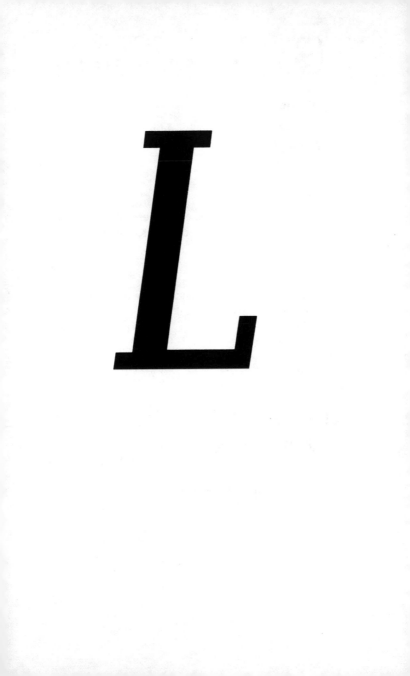

Labour

One of the processes by which A acquires property for B.

Ambrose Bierce

Lady

A word most often used to describe someone you wouldn't want to talk to for even five minutes.

Fran Lebowitz

Someone who never shows her underwear unintentionally.

Lillian Day

A woman who makes a man act like a gentleman.

Russell Lynes

Language

The flowers of afterthought.

Bernard Malamud

A form of organised stutter.

Marshall McLuhan

The felicitous misapplication of words.

J.B. Greenough

Las Vegas

A place with all kinds of gambling devices – roulette tables, slot machines, wedding chapels...

Stanley Davis

Lassitude

When your get up and go has got up and went.

Michael Kennedy

Laughter

The sensation of feeling good all over, and showing it principally in one spot.

Josh Billings

Laws

Spider webs through which the big flies pass and the little ones get caught.

Honoré de Balzac

Lawyer

A learned gentleman who rescues your estate from your enemies...and keeps it for himself.

Lord Brougham

One who protects us from robbers by taking away the temptation.

H.L. Mencken

The Cynic's Dictionary

Someone who'll do anything to win a case —
even tell the truth.

Patrick Murray

Lawyers

People who earn their living by the sweat of
their browbeating.

James Huneker

People who prove that talk definitely isn't
cheap.

Justine McCarthy

Laziness

Riding a bike over cobblestones to knock the
ash off a cigarette.

Les Dawson

Learned Conversation

Either the affectation of the ignorant or the
profession of the mentally unemployed.

Oscar Wilde

Leisure

The opiate of the masses.

Malcolm Muggeridge

Liar

Someone who needs a good memory.

Quintillian

A lawyer with a roving commission.

Ambrose Bierce

Liberal

Someone who tells other people what to do with their money.

Leroi Jones

A conservative who's been arrested.

Thomas Wolfe

A man too broad-minded to take his own side in a quarrel.

Robert Frost

Liberals

People who can understand everything but people who don't understand *them*.

Lenny Bruce

Liberty

The one thing you can't have unless you give it to others.

William A. White

Library

A sort of harem.

Ralph Waldo Emerson

Thought in cold storage.

Lord Herbert Samuel

Polyphemus without an eye in his head.

Thomas Carlyle

The soul's burying ground.

Henry Ward Beecher

Lies

The basic building blocks of good manners.

Quentin Crisp

Life

Something you do when you can't get to sleep.

Fran Lebowitz

A bad dream between two awakenings.

Eugene O'Neill

A game at which everybody loses.

Leo Sarkadi-Schuller

The art of drawing sufficient conclusions from insufficient premises.

Samuel Butler

For most men, a search for the proper manila envelope in which to get themselves filed.

Clifton Fadiman

Not having been told that the man has just waxed the floor.

Ogden Nash

A steady walk with a hidden precipice at the end.

Lambert Jeffries

Post-natal depression.

Nigel Rees

A funny thing that occurs on the way to the grave.

Quentin Crisp

Sobs, sniffles and smiles – with sniffles predominating.

O. Henry

A cheap *table d'hôte* in a rather dirty restaurant, with time changing the plates before you've had enough of anything.

Thomas Kettle

A tragedy when seen in close up, but a comedy in long shot.

Charlie Chaplin

A sexually transmitted disease – and the mortality rate is 100 per cent.

R.D. Laing

A tale told by an idiot, full of sound and fury, signifying nothing.

William Shakespeare

Much too important a thing ever to talk seriously about it.

Oscar Wilde

A maze in which we take the wrong turning before we have learned to walk.

Cyril Connolly

A long rehearsal for a play that's never produced.

Mícheál Mac Liammóir

Literary Agent

Someone you pay to make bad blood between
yourself and your publisher.

Angela Thirkell

Literary Masterpiece

A dictionary out of order.

Jean Cocteau

Literary Movement

Half a dozen writers living in the same country
who detest each other cordially.

George Russell

Literature

Something that's mostly about having sex and
not much about having children – as opposed
to life, which is the other way round.

David Lodge

News that stays news.

Ezra Pound

Proclaiming in front of everybody what one is
careful to conceal from one's immediate circle

Jean Rostand

The question minus the answer.

Roland Barthes

Litter

A disgusting way of proving your affluence.

Sir Henry Bolte

Living

A very time-consuming activity.

Irene Peter

Loafer

Someone who always has the correct time.

Kin Hubbard

Logic

The art of going wrong with confidence.

Joseph Krutch

An instrument used for bolstering a prejudice.

Elbert Hubbard

Neither an art nor a science – but a dodge.

Stendhal

London

A splendid place to live...for those who can get out of it.

Lord Balfour

A hoary, ponderous inferno.

D.H. Lawrence

Chaos incorporated.

George Mikes

Long Island

America's idea of what God would have done with nature if He'd had the money.

Peter Fleming

Longevity

The revenge of talent upon genius.

Cyril Connolly

Loquacity

A disorder which renders the sufferer unable to curb his tongue when you wish to talk.

Ambrose Bierce

Los Angeles

Seventy-two suburbs in search of a city.

Dorothy Parker

The only town in the world where you can
wake up in the morning and listen to the birds
coughing in the trees.

Joe Frisco

A big, hard-boiled city with no more
personality than a paper cup.

Raymond Chandler

Love

What conquers all things – except poverty and
toothache.

Mae West

What has become a four-lettered word.

Fritz Lang

A dirty trick played on us to achieve
continuation of the species.

Somerset Maugham

The extremely difficult realisation that
something other than oneself is real.

Iris Murdoch

Insanity with a collaborator.

Gene Perret

A temporary insanity curable by marriage.

Ambrose Bierce

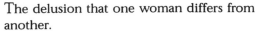
The delusion that one woman differs from another.

> *H.L. Mencken*

Something like the measles – all the worse when it comes late in life.

> *Douglas Jerrold*

The selfishness of two persons.

> *La Salle*

What makes the world go round – but it's spinsters who oil the wheels.

> *Ellen Dorothy Abb*

The wisdom of the fool and the folly of the wise.

> *H.L. Mencken*

Love Affair

A tableau of two wild animals, each with its teeth sunk in the other's neck, each scared to let go in case it bleeds to death.

> *Kenneth Tynan*

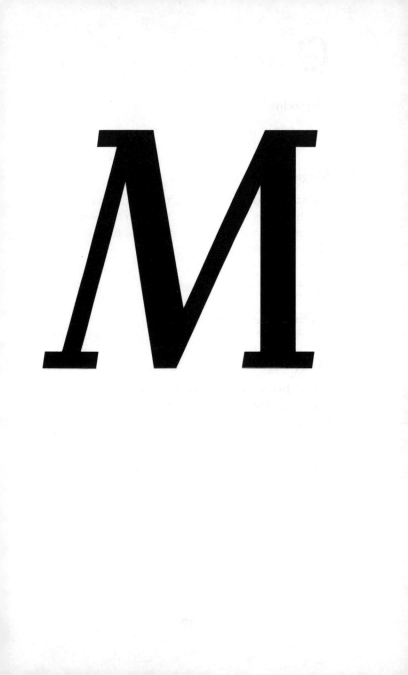

Magazine

The heavy petting of literature.

Fran Lebowitz

Magazine Editor

A man who lives on a sort of spiritual Bataan, with bombs of odium taking him incessantly from the front, and torpedoes of obloquy harrying him astern.

H.L. Mencken

Make-up

What it takes to look natural.

Calvin Klein

Male, The

A domestic animal which, if treated with firmness and kindness, can be trained to do most things.

Jilly Cooper

A useless piece of flesh at the end of a penis.

Jo Brand

The second strangest sex in the world.

Philip Barry

Malice

Like poker or tennis, a game you don't play with anyone who is manifestly inferior to you.

Hilda Spiel

Man

The only animal that can remain on friendly terms with the victims he intends to eat until he eats them.

Samuel Butler

A creature who lives not upon bread alone, but principally by catchwords.

Robert Louis Stevenson

Nature's sole mistake.

W.S. Gilbert

A reasoning rather than a reasonable animal.

Alexander Hamilton

A creature we must laugh at in order to avoid crying for him.

Napoleon

The only animal that blushes – or needs to.

Mark Twain

Management Democracy

Everybody agreeing to do what the leader wants.

John Ashcroft

Manners

The lowest common denominator of ethical experience.

Victor S. Navasky

What are especially the needs of the plain – the pretty can get away with anything.

Evelyn Waugh

Manuscript

Something submitted in haste and returned at leisure.

Oliver Herford

Market Research

What you call it when you already know the answer you want, but still hunt up the question that will produce it.

Robert Fuoss

Marriage

A lot like the army; everyone complains, but you'd be surprised at the large number that re-enlist.

James Garner

Not just a spiritual communion and passionate embraces − but also three meals a day, and remembering to carry out the trash.

Joyce Brothers

A wonderful invention. But then, so is the bicycle repair kit.

Billy Connolly

The only adventure open to the cowardly.

Voltaire

A lottery − but you can't tear up the ticket if you lose.

J.F. Knowles

A book in which the first chapter is written in poetry and the rest in prose.

Beverly Nichols

The first step towards divorce.

Pamela Mason

A triumph of habit over hate.

Oscar Levant

Like paying an endless visit in your worst clothes.

J.B. Priestley

A deal in which a man gives away half his groceries in order to get the other half cooked.

John Gwynne

Where a woman asks a man to remove his pyjamas because she wants to send them to the laundry.

Albert Finney

A man-trap baited with simulated accomplishments and delusive idealisations.

George Bernard Shaw

A licence for two people to insult each other.

Brendan Behan

A bed of roses – but most of them have thorns.

Les Dawson

Legalised rape.

Andrea Dworkin

Neither a verb or a noun, but a sentence.

Revd James Simpson

A bloody impractical institution: if it weren't,
you wouldn't have to sign a contract.

Katharine Hepburn

Martyrdom

The only way a man can become famous
without ability.

George Bernard Shaw

Marxism

Essentially a product of the bourgeois mind.

J. A. Schumpeter

Masses

Breeding grounds of psychic epidemics.

Carl Jung

Masturbation

The thinking man's television.

Christopher Hampton

Sex with someone you love.

Woody Allen

A disease in the nineteenth century; in the
twentieth a *cure*.

Thomas Szasz

Meal-time

The only time in the day when children resolutely refuse to eat.

Fran Lebowitz

When the youngsters continue eating…but sit down.

Herbert Prochnow

Media

A word that has come to mean bad journalism.

Graham Greene

The plural for mediocre.

Rene Saguisag

Medicine

Amusing the patient while nature cures the disease.

Voltaire

Mediocrities

People who are always at their best.

Somerset Maugham

Meetings

Rather like cocktail parties. You don't want to go, but you're cross not to be asked.

Jilly Cooper

What are indispensable when you don't want to do anything.

Kenneth Galbraith

Memoirs

When you put down the good things you ought to have done, and leave out the bad things you *did* do.

Will Rogers

The back stairs of history.

George Meredith

Memorandum

Something that's written not so much to inform the reader as to protect the writer.

Dean Acheson

Memories

Hunting horns whose sound dies on the wind.

Guillaume Appollinaire

Memory

A crazy woman who hoards coloured rags and throws away food.

Austin O'Malley

The thing a man forgets with when he owes you money.

Anthony Butler

What is left when something happens and does not completely unhappen.

Edward de Bono

Men

Portable heaters that snore.

Rita Rudner

Those creatures with two legs and eight hands.

Jayne Mansfield

A great deal of work for very little reward.

Glenda Jackson

Mercedes Benz

A mechanical device that increases sexual arousal in women.

P. J. O'Rourke

Metallurgist

Somebody who can look at a platinum blonde and tell whether she's virgin material or common ore.

Brian Johnston

Metaphysics

An attempt to prove the incredible by an appeal to the unintelligible.

H.L. Mencken

Middle Age

The time of life when the most fun you have is talking about the most fun you used to have.

Gene Perret

The time of your life when, instead of combing your hair, you start 'arranging' it.

Herbert Kavet

When your weightlifting consists merely of standing up.

Bob Hope

When you begin to exchange your emotions for symptoms.

Irvin Cobb

When you're too young to take up golf, and
too old to rush up to the net at tennis.

F. P. Adams

When your medicine chest is better stocked
than your drinks cabinet.

Pam Brown

When a man is always thinking that in a week
or two he will feel as good as ever.

Don Marquis

Having a choice of two temptations and
choosing the one that will get you home
earlier.

Dan Bennett

Middleman

Somebody who plunders one party and
bamboozles the other.

Benjamin Disraeli

Military Intelligence

A contradiction in terms.

Groucho Marx

Mind, The

A woman's most erogenous zone.

Raquel Welch

Minor Operation

One performed on somebody else.

Anon.

Minority Rule

A baby in the house.

Henny Youngman

Miracle

An event described by those to whom it was told by somebody who didn't see it.

Elbert Hubbard

Miracle Drug

Any one that will do what the label says.

Eric Hodgkins

Mirrors

Objects which should think longer before they reflect.

Jean Cocteau

Miser

A man who grows rich by seeming poor.

William Shakespeare

Misfortune

The kind of fortune that never misses.

Ambrose Bierce

Misogynist

A man who hates women as much as women hate each other.

H.L. Mencken

Misprints

The only things that poets can't survive.

Oscar Wilde

Misquotation

The pride and privilege of the learned.

Hesketh Pearson

Missionaries

People who make the world safe for hypocrisy.

Thomas Wolfe

Mistress

Something that comes between the master and the mattress.

Robin Wallis

Mixed Economy

Society in the process of committing suicide.

Ayn Rand

Model Husband

One who, when his wife is away, washes the dishes — both of them.

Herbert Prochnow

Moderation

A virtue only in those who are thought to have an alternative.

Henry Kissinger

Modern Architecture

When you have to keep the lavatory door shut by extending your left leg.

Nancy Banks-Smith

Modern Art

What happens when painters stop looking at girls and persuade themselves that they have a better idea.

John Ciardi

A square lady with three breasts and a guitar up her crotch.

Noel Coward

The Cynic's Dictionary

Modern Music

Three farts and a raspberry, orchestrated.

John Barbirolli

Modern Novels

Literary creations with a beginning, a muddle and an end.

Philip Larkin

Modernity

All signpost and no destination.

Louis Kronenberger

Modesty

The only sure bait when you angle for praise.

Lord Chesterfield

The gentle art of enhancing your charm by pretending not to be aware of it.

Oliver Herford

Monarchy

The gold filling in the mouth of decay.

John Osborne

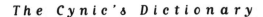

Money

A commodity that's better than poverty, if only for financial reasons.

Woody Allen

The only likeable thing about rich people.

Lady Astor

What you'd get on beautifully without if only other people weren't so crazy about it.

Margaret Herriman

Monogamy

Monotony.

Zsa Zsa Gabor

What leaves a lot to be desired.

Nigel Rees

Monopoly

Business at the end of its journey.

Henry Lloyd

Moral Indignation

What is in most cases 2 per cent moral, 48 per cent indignation, and 50 per cent envy.

Vittorio de Sica

Suspecting other people of not being married.
George Bernard Shaw

Simply the attitude we adopt towards people
we personally dislike.

Oscar Wilde

Motherhood

The most emotional experience of one's life –
one joins a kind of women's mafia.

Janet Suzman

Mourning

Not so much grief at not being able to call the
dead back, as grief at not being able to *want* to
do so.

Thomas Mann

Moustache

The huge laughing cockroach on the top lip.
Osip Mendelstem

Movies

The only business where you can go out front
and applaud yourself.

Will Rogers

The only business where a negative is a
positive.

Menachem Golan

The only court where the judge goes to the
lawyer for advice.

F. Scott Fitzgerald

Muesli

A dish that always looks like the sweepings
from a better class table.

Frank Muir

Murder

Always a mistake: one should never do anything
that one cannot talk about after dinner.

Oscar Wilde

Music

Something invented to confirm human
loneliness.

Lawrence Durrell

The brandy of the damned.

George Bernard Shaw

The most expensive of all noises.

Ralph Hutter

Musical

A series of catastrophes ending with a floorshow.

Oscar Levant

Musical Conductor

A man who has the distinct advantage of not being able to see the audience.

André Kostelanetz

Musicologist

A person who can read music but can't hear it.

Sir Thomas Beecham

Mystics

People who hope that science will one day overtake them.

Booth Tarkington

Myths

Someone else's religion.

Caroline Llewellyn

Gossip grown old.

R.P. Blackmuir

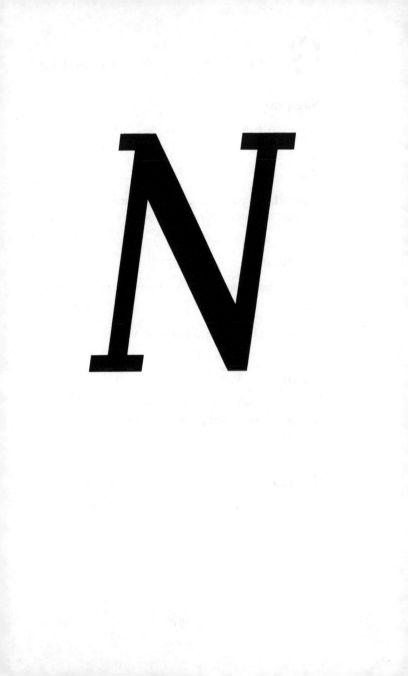

Nagging

The repetition of unpalatable truths.

Edith Summerskill

Nail

Something you aim at before hitting your thumb with the hammer.

Peter Eldin

Narcissist

One who, when he hears thunder, takes a bow.

Louis Safian

Someone better-looking than you are.

Gore Vidal

Nation

A society united by a delusion about its ancestry, and a common hatred of its neighbours.

W.R. Inge

Nationalism

A silly cock crowing on its own dunghill.

Richard Aldington

A political ideology which suggests that every little group of human twerps with its own slang, haircut and pet name for God should have its own country as well.

P.J. O' Rourke

Nature

An immense ruin.

Paul Claudel

Nebraska

Proof that hell is full and the dead walk the earth.

Liz Winston

Necessity

The smotherer of invention.

Lambert Jeffries

God's veil.

Simone Weil

Neighbourhood

A place where, when you go out of it, you get beaten up.

Murray Kempton

 *The Cynic's Dictionary*

Nepotism

Appointing your grandmother to office for the good of the party.

Ambrose Bierce

Net

Anything reticulated or dessucated at equal distances, with interstices between the intersections.

Samuel Johnson

Neurosis

A substitute for legitimate suffering.

Carl Jung

A way of avoiding non-being by avoiding being.

Paul Tillich

Neurotics

People who build castles in the air. (Psychotics live in them, and psychiatrists collect the rent.)

Lord Webb

Those who founded our religions and created our masterpieces.

Marcel Proust

New York

America's thyroid gland.

Christopher Morley

A third rate Babylon.

H.L. Mencken

The only city in the world where you can get deliberately run over on the sidewalk by a pedestrian.

Russell Baker

A city so decadent that when I leave it I never dare to look back lest I turn into salt, and the conductor throw me over his left shoulder for good luck.

Frank Sullivan

That unnatural city where everyone is an exile, none more so than the American.

Charlotte Gilman

New Zealand

A country of thirty million sheep, three million of whom think they're human beings.

Barry Humphries

News

What a chap who doesn't care much about anything wants to read.

Evelyn Waugh

The first rough draft of history.

Ben Bradlee

Newspaper

A device unable to distinguish between a bicycle accident and the collapse of civilisation.

George Bernard Shaw

An object used by tired men to avoid seeing a woman standing on a bus.

Herbert Prochnow

Newspaper Paragraphing

The art of stroking a platitude until it purrs like an epigram.

Don Marquis

Nickname

The heaviest stone that the devil can throw at a man.

William Hazlitt

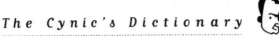
Nightclubs

Places where the tables are reserved but the guests aren't.

Frank Caspar

Non-conformity

The new conformity.

T.S. Eliot

Nonsense

A good thing because common sense is so limited.

George Santayana

Nostalgia

A seductive liar.

George Ball

A thing of the past.

Janet Rogers

Novelist

A historian of conscience.

Frederic Raphael

Numbers

The only universal language.

Nathaniel West

Nurses

Women who are full of cheerfulness over other people's troubles.

Agatha Christie

Nymphomaniac

A woman who thinks about sex as much as the average man.

Mignon McLaughlin

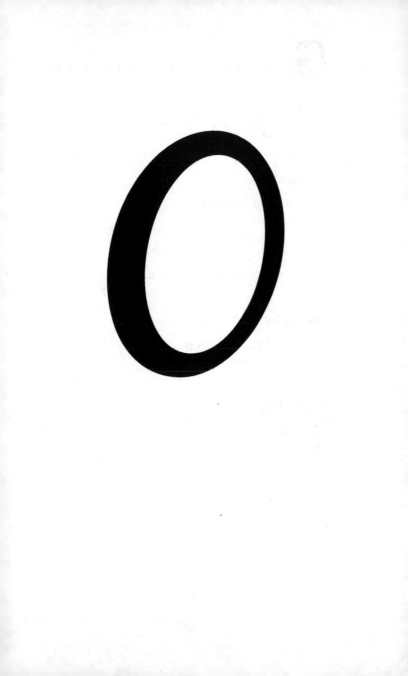

Oaths

The fossils of piety.

George Santayana

Obesity

A widespread ailment.

Joseph Kern

Obituary

The only kind of bad publicity for a writer.

Brendan Behan

Obscenity

Whatever happens to shock some elderly and ignorant magistrate.

Bertrand Russell

Ocean Racing

Like standing under a cold shower tearing up £5 notes.

Edward Heath

October

One of the peculiarly dangerous months in which to speculate in stocks. The others are January, February, March, April, May, June, July, August, September, November and December.

Mark Twain

Octopus

An eight-sided cat.

Kevin Goldstein-Jackson

Office Hours

Two to 2.15 every other Wednesday.

George Kaufman

Old Age

A lot of crossed-off names in an address book.

Ronald Blythe

A very high price to pay for maturity.

Tom Stoppard

Always 15 years older than what I am.

Bernard Baruch

Not so bad when you consider the alternative.

Maurice Chevalier

Life's parody.

Simone de Beauvoir

When you try to straighten the wrinkles on your socks and discover you're not wearing any.

Leonard Knott

The period of life in which we compensate for the vices that remain by reviling those we have no longer the vigour to commit.

Ambrose Bierce

Old-timer

Someone who remembers when a family went for a drive on Sunday afternoon and everyone got into the same car.

Stanley Davis

Someone who gives good advice in order to console himself for no longer being able to set a bad example.

Duc de La Rochefoucauld

Old-fashioned Marriage

One that outlasts the wedding gifts.

Hal Roach

Opening Night

The night before a play is ready to open.

George Jean Nathan

Opera

When a guy gets stabbed in the back and, instead of bleeding, he sings.

Ed Gardner

Opinion Poll

A survey which claims to show what voters are thinking, but which only succeeds in changing their minds.

Miles Kington

Opportunist

A person who strikes a 50-50 deal in such a way that he insists on getting the hyphen as well.

Jack Benny

Opportunities

Things usually disguised as hard work so most people don't recognise them.

Ann Landers

Optimism

The digitalis of failure.

Elbert Hubbard

The contentment of small men in high places.

F. Scott Fitzgerald

Optimist

Someone who hasn't got around to reading the morning papers.

Earl Wilson

Someone who tells you to cheer up when things are going his way.

Edward Murrow

One who fills up his crossword puzzle in ink.

Clement King Shorter

A man who gets married at 93 and buys a house near a school.

Stanley Davis

Oratory

The art of making a loud noise like a deep thought.

Bennett Cerf

Original Sin

The only original thing about some men.

Helen Rowland

Original Thought

Like original sin – both happened before you were born, to people you could not have possibly met.

Fran Lebowitz

Originality

The fine art of remembering what you heard, but forgetting where you heard it.

Laurence Peter

Orgasm

What has replaced the cross as the focus of longing and the image of fulfillment.

Malcolm Muggeridge

Orthodoxy

Yesterday's heresy.

Helen Keller

Ourselves

The people our mothers warned us against.

John Lennon

Outdoors, The

What you must pass through in order to get
from your apartment to a taxi-cab.

Fran Lebowitz

Over-eating

The most worthy of sins: it neither breaks up
marriages nor causes road accidents.

Richard Condon

Oxford

Like a chat show, but with more people.

Alan Coren

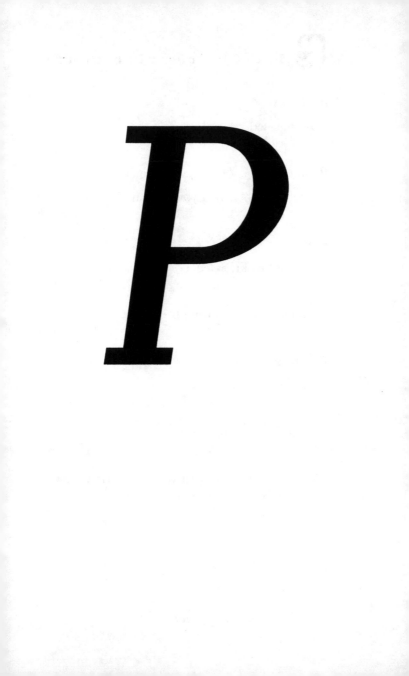

Pacifism

Undisguised cowardice.

Adolf Hitler

Pagan

What you get when you scratch a Christian.

Israel Zangwill

Pain

The root of knowledge.

Simone Weil

Nature's way of getting back.

Audrey Austin

Painting

The Bible of the laity.

Gratian

A blind man's profession.

Pablo Picasso

An activity that's easy if you don't know how to do it, but difficult when you do.

Edgar Degas

Pantomime

The smell of wee-wee and oranges.

Tommy Trinder

Papacy, The

The ghost of the deceased Roman Empire, sitting crowned upon the grave thereof.

Thomas Hobbes

Parenthood

That state of being better chaperoned than you were before marriage.

Marcelene Cox

Parents

Those who are sometimes a bit of a disappointment to their children, having failed to fulfil the promise of their early years.

Anthony Powell

People who were invented to make children happy by giving them something to ignore.

Ogden Nash

Paris

Where good Americans go to when they die.

Ogden Nash

A city asleep - and snoring loudly.

Ned Rorem

Parks

Pavements disguised with a growth of grass.

George Gissing

Parties

Fêtes worse than death.

Barbara Stanwyck

Pas de Deux

Father of twins.

Janet Rogers

Passport

A document treacherously inflicted upon a citizen going abroad, exposing him as an alien and pointing him out for special reprobation and outrage.

Ambrose Bierce

Passport Picture

Something that, when you look like it, it's time to go home.

Erma Bombeck

Passion

The desire to take a cigarette out of one's mouth before kissing one's betrothed.

Gary Davies

Patience

The willingness to listen to the other person tell you his troubles before you tell him yours.

Herbert Prochnow

A minor form of despair, disguised as a virtue.

Ambrose Bierce

A willingness to hold the umbrella over a man's head while he changes a wheel.

Katharine Whitehorn

Patriotism

An arbitrary veneration of real estate above principles.

George Jean Nathan

The willingness to kill and be killed for trivial reasons.

Bertrand Russell

The conviction that your country is superior to all others because you were born in it.

George Bernard Shaw

The last refuge of a scoundrel.

Samuel Johnson

Not only the last refuge of a scoundrel, but the first bolt-hole of the hypocrite.

Melvin Bragg

Patriots

People who always talk of dying for their country, but never of *killing* for it.

Bertrand Russell

Patron

A wretch who supports with insolence, and is paid with flattery.

Samuel Johnson

Pauses

The most precious things in speeches.

Ralph Richardson

Peace

In international affairs, a period of cheating between two periods of fighting.

Ambrose Bierce

Not only better than war, but infinitely more arduous.

George Bernard Shaw

A continuation of war by other means.

Vo Nguyen Giap

Pedantry

The dotage of knowledge.

Holbrook Jackson

Stupidity that read a book.

Samuel Butler

Pedestrians

People who are knocked down by motor cars.

J.B. Morton

Pen

What is mightier than the sword – and considerably easier to write with.

Marty Feldman

Penitent

Someone who feels remorse for what he did yesterday and what he's going to do again tomorrow.

Anon.

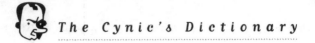

Pentagon, The

A building in America that has five sides...on every issue.

Hal Roach

Peptic Ulcer

A hole in a man's stomach through which he crawls to escape from his wife.

J.A.D. Anderson

Permissiveness

Removing the dust sheets from our follies.

Edna O'Brien

Pessimist

A man who has been compelled to live with an optimist.

Elbert Hubbard

A man who thinks everyone is as nasty as himself and hates them for it.

George Bernard Shaw

A man who looks both ways before crossing a one-way street.

Robert Lowell

Someone who burns his bridges before he gets to them.

Anon.

A man who thinks all women are bad.
(An optimist is one who hopes they are!)

Chauncey Depew

Philanthropist

A rich and usually bald old gentleman who has trained himself to grin while his conscience is picking his pocket.

Ambrose Bierce

A parasite on misery.

George Bernard Shaw

Philanthropy

The refuge of people who wish to annoy their fellow creatures.

Oscar Wilde

Philistine

A term of contempt applied by prigs to the rest of their species.

Sir Leslie Stephen

Philosopher

Someone with a problem for every solution.
Robert Zend

Somebody who doesn't care for philosophy.
Blaise Pascal

Philosophy

To the real world what masturbation is to sex.
Karl Marx

Unintelligible answers to insoluble problems.
Henry Adams

Common sense in a dress suit.
Oliver Braston

Language idling.
Ludwig Wittgenstein

Despair's shot at happiness.
Alexander Pope

Photography

The art form of the untalented.
Gore Vidal

Brothels without walls.
Marshall McLuhan

Pickpockets

The nearest thing I have to a sex life these days.

Rodney Dangerfield

Picture

Something between a thing and a thought.

Samuel Palmer

Plagiarists

People who are always suspicious of being stolen from.

Samuel Taylor Coleridge

Planned Economy

When everything is included in the plans...except economy.

Carey McWilliams

Platitude

A truth repeated until people get tired of hearing it.

Stanley Baldwin

Platonic Friendship

The interval between the introduction and the first kiss.

Sophie Loeb

Playboy

A man who believes in wine, women and so-long.

John Travolta

Somebody who's tall, dark and hands.

Henny Youngman

Playwrights

People who should be dead for 300 years.

Joseph L. Mankiewicz

Poem

What happens when anxiety meets technique.

Lawrence Durrell

A prolonged hesitation between sound and sense.

Paul Valery

Poetry

An activity like dropping a rose petal into the Grand Canyon and waiting for the echo.

Don Marquis

Not just when the lines fail to reach the end of the page.

Leonard Cohen

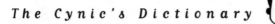

An impish attempt to paint the colour of the wind.

Maxwell Bodenheim

A comforting piece of fiction set to more or less lascivious music.

H.L. Mencken

The devil's wine.

Saint Augustine

A form of refrigeration that stops language going bad.

Peter Porter

Religion without hope.

Jean Cocteau

What Milton saw when he went blind.

Don Marquis

Cissy stuff that rhymes.

Geoffrey Williams

Poetry Books

Handy implements for killing persistent irritating flies.

Geoffrey Grigson

Poets

People who are usually dead by their late twenties.

Robert Graves

Poise

The ability to keep talking while someone else picks up the cheque.

Jack Benny

Poker

A game that shouldn't be played in a house with women.

Tennessee Williams

Police Files

Our only claim to immortality.

Milan Kundera

Politeness

Mankind's most acceptable hypocrisy.

Ambrose Bierce

Organised indifference.

Paul Valery

Not speaking evil of people with whom you have just dined until you are at least a hundred yards from their house.

André Maurois

The art of choosing among one's real thoughts.

Abel Stevens

Political Asylum

Any governmental office.

Johnny Carson

Politician

A person with whose politics you don't agree. (If you agree with him, he's a statesman.)

David Lloyd George

An animal that can sit on the fence and still keep both ears to the ground.

H.L. Mencken

A fellow who will lay down your life for his country.

Texas Guinan

One who approaches every situation with an open mouth.

Adlai Stevenson

Someone who believes you don't have to fool the people all the time – just during election campaigns.

Stanley Davis

Politicians

People who divide their time between running for office and running for cover.

Anon.

People who shake your *hand* before an election, and your confidence after.

Ernie Kovacs

People who, when they see the light at the end of the tunnel, order more tunnel.

John Quintan

Politics

The sport of rich men and prostitutes.

Richard Dreyfuss

An occupation that has become so expensive, it takes a lot of money even to be defeated.

Will Rogers

The only profession for which no preparation is thought necessary.

Robert Louis Stevenson

Choosing between the disastrous and the unpalatable.

J.K. Galbraith

A dog's life without a dog's decencies.

Rudyard Kipling

A science derived from two words: 'poli' meaning many, and 'tics' meaning small bloodsucking insects.

Chris Clayton

Poll

Where people come to their census.

Anon.

Ponder

To arrive at a stupid conclusion slowly.

Herbert Prochnow

Popularity

A crime from the moment it's sought.

George Savile Halifax

The Cynic's Dictionary

Portrait

A painting with something wrong with the mouth.

John Singer Sargent

Posterity

What you write for after being rejected by all the reputable publishers.

George Ade

Poverty

Something that's very good in poetry but very bad in the house.

Henry Ward Beecher

Power

The ultimate aphrodisiac.

Henry Kissinger

Power Politics

The diplomatic name for the law of the jungle.

Ely Culbertson

P.R. Counsellor

A press agent with a manicure.

Alan Gordon

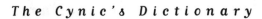

Praying

When you talk to God. Not to be cofused with schizophrenia, which is when He talks back.

Lily Tomlin

The most odious form of concealed narcissism.

John Fowles

Pregnancy

What, if it were a book, they'd cut out the last two chapters.

Nora Ephron

Prejudices

The props of civilisation.

André Gide

The reason of fools.

Voltaire

Preposition

Something you should never end a sentence with.

Jill Etherington

Present, The

The now, the here, through which all future plunges to the past.

James Joyce

Prison

The poor man's boarding school.

Brendan Behan

Private School

A place which has all the faults of a public one, without any of its compensations.

Cyril Connolly

Problems

Opportunities in work clothes.

Henry H. Kaiser

Procrastination

The art of keeping up with yesterday.

Don Marquis

A longer word for laziness.

Danny Cummins

Putting off until tomorrow what you put off yesterday until today.

Laurence Peter

Prodigy

A child who plays the piano when he ought to be in bed.

J.B. Morton

Producers

People who should give ulcers rather than get them.

Samuel Goldwyn

Professor

One who talks in someone else's sleep.

W.H. Auden

Progress

The exchange of one nuisance for another.

Havelock Ellis

A wonderful thing – if only it would stop.

Robert Musil

Planned obsolescence.

Jeffrey Roche

Promoters

Guys with two pieces of bread looking for the same cheese.

Evel Knievel

Propaganda

A monologue which seeks not a response, but an echo.

W.H. Auden

The art of persuading others of what one does not believe oneself.

Abba Eban

That branch of the art of lying which consists in nearly deceiving your friends while not quite deceiving your enemies.

F.M. Cornford

Property

Organised robbery.

George Bernard Shaw

Prosperity

Something which, like perfume, often makes the head ache.

Margaret Cavendish

Protestantism

A religion which has as its chief contribution to human thought the massive proof that God is a bore.

H.L. Mencken

Psychiatrist

A man who asks you a lot of expensive questions your wife will ask you for nothing.

Sam Bardell

A man who goes to a strip show to watch the audience.

Mervyn Stockwood

A sex maniac who failed the practicals.

Milton Berle

Psychiatrists

People one should only see out of boredom.

Muriel Spark

Psychiatry

A process of putting two and two together and then trying to figure out why the answer wasn't four.

Dr Hillis Owen

A form of horizontal confession subscribed to by those who would like to know why they do things that have always been done.

Hal Roach

Psychoanalysis

Confession without absolution.

G.K.Chesterton

Psychologist

Someone you go to when you're slightly cracked, and continue attending until you're totally broke.

Tony Hancock

Psychology

The theory that the patient will probably get well anyhow, and is certainly a damned fool.

H.L. Mencken

Public Life

The paradise of voluble windbags.

George Bernard Shaw

Public Opinion

A compound of folly, weakness, prejudice, wrong feeling, right feeling, obstinacy and newspaper paragraphs.

Sir Robert Peel

A vulgar, impertinent, anonymous tyrant who deliberately makes life unpleasant for anyone who is not content to be the average man.

W.R. Inge

Public Relations

Organised lying.

Lord Wilson

Public Schoolboy

Someone who must be acceptable at a dance – and invaluable in a shipwreck.

Alan Bennett

Publication

The male equivalent of childbirth.

Richard Acland

Publishers

People who kill good trees to put out bad newspapers.

James G. Watt

Publishing

The self-invasion of privacy.

Marshall McLuhan

Pun

The lowest form of wit – unless you thought of it first.

Oscar Levant

Punctuality

The virtue of the bored.

Evelyn Waugh

The art of arriving for an appointment just in time to be indignant at the lateness of other people.

Herbert Prochnow

If you're there before it's over.

James J. Walker

Something that, if you have it, nobody is ever around to appreciate it.

Hylda Baker

Puritan

A person who pours righteous indignation into the wrong things.

G.K. Chesterton

Puritanism

The haunting fear that someone, somewhere may be happy.

H.L. Mencken

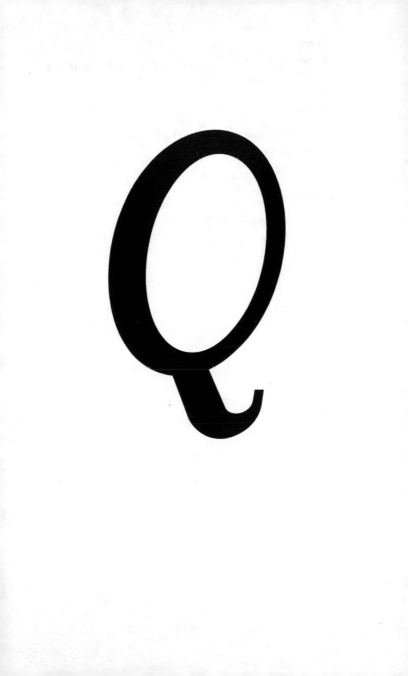

Quartet

Four men, all of whom think the other three can't sing.

Herbert Prochnow

Quietness

A conversation with an Englishman.

Heinrich Heine

Quoting

The act of repeating erroneously the words of another.

Ambrose Bierce

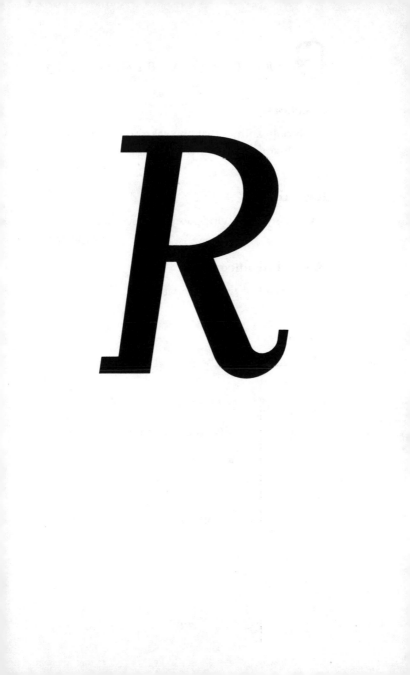

Racehorse

The only animal that can take thousands of people for a ride at the same time.

Herbert Prochnow

Race Track

A place where windows clean people.

Henny Youngman

Racial Prejudice

A pigment of the imagination.

Nigel Rees

Racism

The snobbery of the poor.

Raymond Aron

Racist

Somebody who wins an argument with a liberal.

Peter Brimelow

Radical

A man with both feet planted firmly in the air.

F.D. Roosevelt

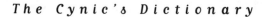

Someone who becomes a conservative on the day after the revolution.

Hannah Arendt

A person whose left hand doesn't know what his other left hand is doing.

Bernard Rosenberg

Radio

Death in the afternoon – and into the night.

Arthur Miller

Rain

What makes flowers grow – and taxis disappear.

Hal Roach

Something that, when you carry an umbrella, it doesn't.

Laurence Peter

Rationalisation

Replacing the tea-lady with a vending machine.

Mitchell Symons

Reactionary

A somnambulist walking backwards.

Franklin D. Roosevelt

Reader

Someone who comes under the protection of
the Endangered Species Act.

Dennis Potter

Reading

An ashamed way of killing time disguised
under a dignified name.

Ernest Dimnet

An ingenious device for drugging thought.

Sir Arthur Helps

Reality

An illusion created by the lack of alcohol.

N.F. Simpson

A crutch for people who can't cope with drugs.

Lily Tomlin

Reason

Emotion for the sexless.

Alfred North Whitehead

Recession

When a neighbour loses his job – as opposed
to depression, which is when you lose yours.

Ronald Reagan

Reformer

A guy who rides through a sewer in a glass-bottomed boat.

James J. Walker

Regeneration

What every generation needs.

C.H. Spurgeon

Regret

A woman's natural food, upon which she thrives.

Sir Arthur Pinero

Reincarnation

An ideology that's making a comeback.

Simon O'Connor

Relationships

Things we get into just to get out of the ones we're not brave enough to say are over.

Julia Phillips

Religion

A practice comparable to a childhood neurosis.

Sigmund Freud

A monumental chapter in the history of human egotism.

William James

A belief that the gods are on the side of the government.

Bertrand Russell

The venereal disease of mankind.

Henri de Montherlant

A fashionable substitute for belief.

Oscar Wilde

Excellent stuff for keeping common people quiet.

Napoleon

Re-marriage

An excellent way to test just how amicable your divorce was.

Margo Kaufman

Remorse

Pride's substitute for repentance.

Aldous Huxley

Repartee

What you wished you'd said after you didn't.
Heywood Broun

A duel fought with the points of jokes.
Max Eastman

Repentance

Want of power to sin.
John Dryden

Reporter

A man who has renounced everything in life
but the world, the flesh and the devil.
David Murray

Research

The process of going up alleys to see if they're
blind.
Marston Bates

What I'm doing when I don't know what I'm
doing.
Wernher von Braun

Resentment

Resting on one's quarrels.
Vida Shiffrer

Resolutions

Cheques that men draw on a bank where they have no account.

Oscar Wilde

Restaurant

The only place where people are happy to be fed up.

Hal Roach

Mouth brothels.

Frederic Raphael

Retirement

The ugliest word in the language.

Ernest Hemingway

Twice the husband on half the money.

Sean McCarthy

Revenge

A dish that tastes better cold.

Anon.

Revivals

Shallow things, because they aim at reproducing what never existed, or what has perished with the age that gave them birth.

W.R. Inge

Revolution

A trivial shift in the emphasis of suffering.

Tom Stoppard

An attempt to substitute misrule for bad government.

Anthony Butler

Revolutionary

Someone who ends up either as an oppressor or a heretic.

Albert Camus

Rhubarb

The vegetable of stomach ache.

Ambrose Bierce

Rich People

The scum of the earth in every country.

G.K. Chesterton

Just poor people with money.

Bridget O'Donnell

Robbery

The price charged for any article abroad.

J.B. Morton

Rock and Roll

The sound of grown men throwing tantrums.

Bono

Rock Journalism

People who can't write, interviewing people who can't talk, for people who can't read.

Frank Zappa

Romans, The

A race of people who would never have found the time to conquer the world if they had first been obliged to learn Latin.

Heinrich Heine

Rut

A grave with the ends knocked out.

Laurence Peter

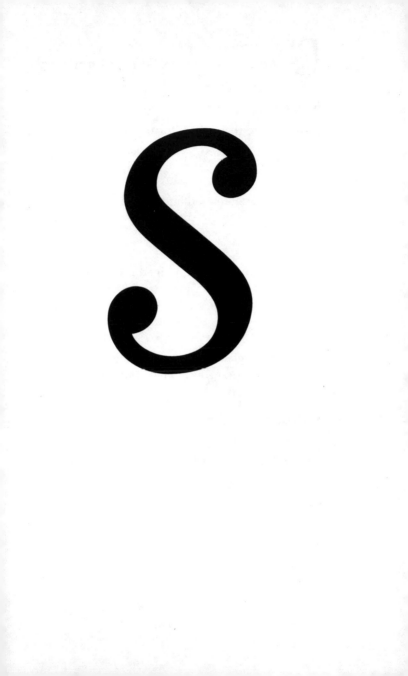

Sadness

An appetite that no misfortune can satisfy.

E.M. Cioran

Saint

A dead sinner, revised and edited.

Ambrose Bierce

Saints

People who should be judged guilty until proven innocent.

George Orwell

Satire

The sort of glass, wherein beholders do generally discover everybody's face but their own.

Jonathan Swift

Satirist

A man who discovers unpleasant things about himself and then says them about other people.

Peter McArthur

Sausages

Breadcrumbs in battle dress.

Tommy Handley

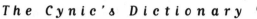

Scandal

The passionate allowance which the gay make to the humdrum.

Saki

Scepticism

The beginning of faith.

Oscar Wilde

The chastity of the intellect.

George Santayana

The first step on the road to philosophy.

Diderot

Scholar

An idler who kills time with study.

George Bernard Shaw

Science

A collection of successful recipes.

Paul Valéry

The art of systematic over-simplification.

Karl Popper

The topography of ignorance.

Oliver Wendell Holmes Jnr.

The Cynic's Dictionary

Science Fiction

The archaeology of the future.

Clifton Fadiman

Scientists

Peeping Toms at the keyhole of eternity.

Arthur Koestler

Scoundrel

Every man over forty.

George Bernard Shaw

Screenwriting

An occupation akin to stuffing kapok in mattresses.

S.J. Perelman

Sculpture

Mud pies which endure.

Cyril Connolly

Self-denial

Not a virtue; only the effect of prudence on rascality.

George Bernard Shaw

The shining sore on the leprous body of Christianity.

Oscar Wilde

Self-evaluation

The skin rash of the emotionally insecure.

John MacDonald

Self-love

The greatest of all flatterers.

Duc de La Rochefoucauld

Self-made Man

One who believes in luck…and sends his son to Oxford.

Christina Stead

Self-respect

The secure feeling that no one, as yet, is suspicious.

H.L. Mencken

Sense of Humour

The ability to be able to laugh at your own jokes when your wife tells them.

Leopold Fechtner

Sentimentalist

One who desires to have the luxury of an emotion without paying for it.

Oscar Wilde

Sentimentality

A superstructure covering brutality.

Carl Jung

The bank holiday of cynicism.

Oscar Wilde

Seriousness

The only refuge of the shallow.

Oscar Wilde

Sermons

Like pie-crusts: the shorter the better.

Austin O'Malley

Sex

The invention of a very clever venereal disease.

David Cronenberg

The poor man's polo.

Clifford Odets

One of the nine reasons for reincarnation. The other eight aren't important.

Henry Miller

What's allowed in Scotland only when Rangers beat Celtic.

Ronnie Barker

An emotion in motion.

Mae West

An activity a bit like asking someone to blow your nose for you.

Philip Larkin

God's joke on human beings.

Bette Davis

The only game that becomes less interesting when played for money.

Anon.

The only game that is never called off on account of darkness.

Laurence Peter

The most fun you can have without laughing.

Woody Allen

The last important human activity not subject to taxation.

Russell Barker

Shame

The feeling you have when you agree with the woman who loves you that you are the man she thinks you are.

Carl Sandburg

Shock Treatment

When the psychiatrist gives you the bill in advance.

Harry Hershfield

Silence

The virtue of fools.

Francis Bacon

One of the hardest arguments to refute.

Josh Billings

That unbearable repartee.

G.K. Chesterton

The most precious thing in a speech.

Ralph Richardson

The most perfect expression of scorn.

George Bernard Shaw

Silk

Material invented so women could go naked in clothes.

Muhammad

Sixty

The age at which one starts to get young – but by then it's too late.

Pablo Picasso

Ski-ing

An activity that combines outdoor fun with knocking down trees with your face.

Dave Barry

Skid Row

A place where a cat with a tail is considered a tourist.

Rachel Waldron

Slang

A language that rolls up its sleeves, spits on its hands and goes to work.

Carl Sandburg

The poor man's poetry.

John Moore

Sleep

When all the unsorted stuff comes flying out from a dustbin upset in a high wind.

William Golding

An excellent way of listening to an opera.

James Stephens

Death without the responsibility.

Fran Lebowitz

Smoking

One of the leading causes of statistics.

Fletcher Knebel

Snobs

Those who talk as if they had begotten their own ancestors.

Herbert Agar

Snobbery

The pride of those who aren't sure of their position.

Berton Braley

Society

A hospital for incurables.

Ralph Waldo Emerson

Sociology

The science with the greatest number of methods and the least results.

J.H. Poincare

The study of people who don't need to be studied...by those who do.

E.S. Turner

Solicitor

A man who calls in a person he doesn't know, to sign a contract he hasn't seen, to buy property he doesn't want, with money he hasn't got.

Dingwall Bateson

Solitude

The playfield of Satan.

Vladimir Nabokov

A luxury of the rich.

Albert Camus

Solutions

The chief causes of problems.

Peter Dickson

Solvency

Making enough money to pay the taxes you wouldn't have to pay if you weren't making so much money.

Vern McLellan

Sophistication

The ability to yawn without opening your mouth.

Herbert Prochnow

Sorrow

Tranquillity remembered in emotion.

Dorothy Parker

Specialist

A man who knows more and more about less and less.

William James Mayo

A man who knows everything about something and nothing about anything else.

Ambrose Bierce

Specialists

People who tend to think in grooves.

Elaine Morgan

Speech

An invention of man's to keep him from thinking.

Agatha Christie

Speed

The one genuinely modern pleasure.

Aldous Huxley

Spendthrift

One who makes his heirs grey.

Joel Rothman

Spice

The plural of spouse.

Christopher Morley

Spinsterhood

Like death by drowning – a delightful sensation after you cease to struggle.

Edna Ferber

Spoon-feeding

An activity which, in the long run, teaches us nothing but the shape of the spoon.

E.M. Forster

Stability

Having a chip on both shoulders.

Mary Mannion

Stardom

The ability to get insulted in places the average negro could never hope to get insulted.

Sammy Davis Jnr

A dull, aching euphoria. You have no friends: you have *disciples*.

Robert Mitchum

Starlet

Any girl under thirty in Hollywood who is not regularly employed in a brothel.

Ben Hecht

Statisticians

A bit like alienists: they will testify to either side.

Fiorello La Guardia

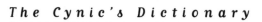

Those who can go directly from an unwarranted assumption to a preconceived conclusion.

Herbert Prochnow

Statistics

Like a bikini: what they reveal is suggestive, but what they conceal is vital.

Aaron Levenstein

Figures that can prove anything – even the truth.

Noel Moynihan

Figures that prove the best time to buy anything was last year.

Jack Benny

Stigma

Something you beat a dogma with.

Philip Guedalla

Stockbroker

A man who can take a bankroll and run it into a shoestring.

Alexander Woollcott

Style

Knowing who you are, what you want to say,
and not giving a damn.

Gore Vidal

When they're running you out of town and
you make it look as if you're leading a parade.

William Battie

Self-plagiarism.

Alfred Hitchcock

Suburbia

Where developers bulldoze trees, and then
name the streets after them.

Bill Vaughan

Success

What's counted sweetest by those who ne'er
succeed.

Emily Dickinson

The ability to torture a higher class of person.

Sharon Stone

Something that's made a failure of many men.

Cindy Adams

As lonely and ice-cold as the North Pole.

Vicki Baum

Being bored by those who used to snub you.

Nancy Astor

Delayed failure.

Graham Greene

Failure disguised as money.

Brendan Behan

The only infallible criterion of wisdom to vulgar minds.

Edmund Burke

Never having to admit you're unhappy.

Robert Evans

Successful Man

One who makes more money than his wife can spend – and a successful woman is one who can find such a man.

Lana Turner

Suicide

Belated acquiescence in the opinion of one's wife's relatives.

H.L. Mencken

 *The Cynic's Dictionary*

Supermarket

A place where you can find anything…except your children.

Leopold Fechtner

Sunday

A day given over by Americans to wishing that they themselves were dead and in Heaven and that their neighbours were dead and in Hell.

H. L. Mencken

Survival

The ultimate revenge.

Vincent Browne

Sunday School

A prison in which children do penance for the evil conscience of their parents.

H.L. Mencken

Swearing

Something invented as a compromise between running away and fighting.

Finley Peter Dunne

Swiss, The

Not so much a people as a neat, clean, quite solvent business.

William Faulkner

Switzerland

A large, humpy solid rock with a thin skin of grass stretched over it.

Mark Twain

A country of phobic handwashers living in a giant Barclays Bank.

Jonathan Raban

The land of peace, understanding, milk chocolate...and all those lovely snow-capped tax benefits.

David Niven

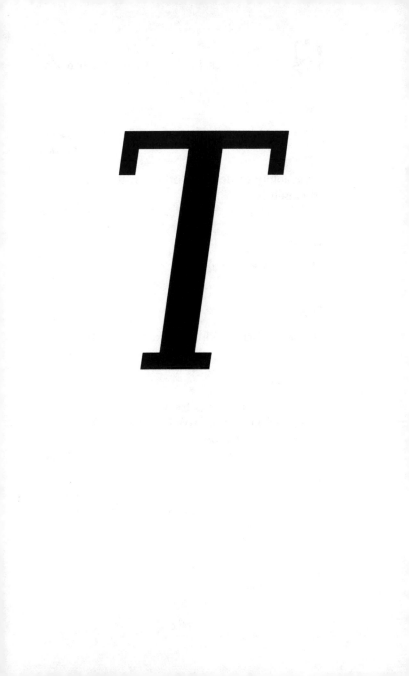

Tact

The art of knowing how far we may go too far.

Jean Cocteau

The ability to describe others as they see themselves.

Abraham Lincoln

Talking

The disease of age.

Desmond Larkin

Tavern

A place where madness is sold by the bottle.

Jonathan Swift

Taxpayer

Someone who works for the federal government, but doesn't have to take a civil service examination.

Ronald Reagan

Teaching

An activity that has ruined more American novelists than drink.

Gore Vidal

One-fourth preparation and three-fourths theatre.

Gail Godwin

The last refuge of feeble minds with classical education.

Aldous Huxley

Team Spirit

An illusion that you only glimpse when you win.

Steve Archibald

Tears

A woman's rhetoric.

Joseph Jordan

Technology

The knack of so arranging the world that we don't have to experience it.

Max Frisch

Teenagers

Boys who'll walk ten miles in a protest parade, but when they're home want to ride their motorcycles from the bedroom to the breakfast table.

Stanley Davis

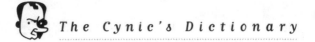

Teens, The

The last stage of your life when you'll be happy to hear the phone is for you.

Fran Lebowitz

Television

An invention that permits you to be entertained in your living-room by people you wouldn't have in your home.

David Frost

A device that permits people who haven't anything to do to watch people who can't do anything.

Fred Allen

Democracy at its ugliest.

Paddy Chayevsky

The longest amateur night in history.

Robert Carson

A medium – because it is neither rare nor well done.

Ernie Kovacs

Something one should appear on, not look at.

Noel Coward

A medium that has brought murder back into
the home, where it belongs.

Alfred Hitchcock

A form of entertainment which permits
millions of people to listen to the same
joke at the same time and yet remain lonesome.

T.S. Eliot

An ugly piece of furniture.

John Waters

Where old movies go when they die.

Bob Hope

Nature's way of telling us we should have gone
out and done something enjoyable.

Gene Perret

Television Acting

Like being asked by the captain to entertain the
passengers while the ship goes down.

Peter Ustinov

Television Sponsor

A guy who watches the commercials and goes
to the fridge during the show.

Stanley Davis

The Cynic's Dictionary

Theatre

The aspirin of the middle classes.

Wolcott Gibbs

A place where lying is looked upon as an occupational disease.

Tallulah Bankhead

Theology

The effort to explain the unknowable in terms of the not worth knowing.

H.L. Mencken

Thinking

A momentary dismissal of irrelevancies.

R. Buckminster Fuller

Thirty

A nice age for a woman – especially if she happens to be forty.

Phyllis Diller

Three O'clock

The time of day when it's always too late or too early for anything you want to do.

Jean-Paul Sartre

Throne

Only a bench covered with velvet.

Napoleon

Time

What man is always trying to kill, but which ends in killing him.

Herbert Spencer

An accordion with all the air being squeezed out of it as you grow older.

Helen Santmyer

What wounds all heels.

Jane Ace

Money.

Benjamin Franklin

Tip

A small sum of money you give to someone because you're afraid he wouldn't like not being paid for something you haven't asked him to do.

Ann Caesar

Today

The tomorrow you worried about yesterday.

Mort Sahl

Tolerance

The virtue of a man without convictions.

G.K. Chesterton

Tourist

A man who travels hundreds of miles just to get a photograph of himself standing beside his car.

Hal Roach

Tragedy

Brutalised farce.

Gordon Craig

Undeveloped comedy.

Paddy Kavanagh

Travel

What's only glamorous in retrospect.

Paul Theroux

The process of journeying thousands of miles
away from people to avoid them, and then
sending them a card saying, 'Wishing you
were here'.

E.C. McKenzie

Trial

A formal inquiry designed to prove and put
upon record the blameless characters of judges,
advocates and jurors.

Ambrose Bierce

Trip

What you take when you can't take any more
of what you've been taking.

Adeline Ainsworth

Troubles

Like babies, things that only grow by nursing.

Douglas Jerrold

Truths

Things that usually begin as blasphemies.

George Bernard Shaw

Tyranny

What is always better organised than freedom.

Charles Péguy

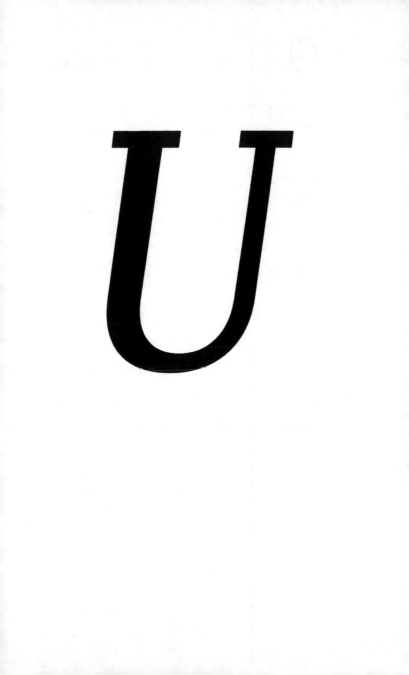

Unconventionality

Really the most conventional convention.

R.H. Benson

Undertaker

The last man to let you down.

Jimmy O'Dea

Undeserved Praise

Satire in disguise.

Alexander Pope

Unhealthy

What thin people call fat people – and vice versa.

Sandra Bergeson

University

What a college becomes when the faculty loses interest in its students.

John Ciardi

A place where they polish pebbles and dim diamonds.

Sean O'Casey

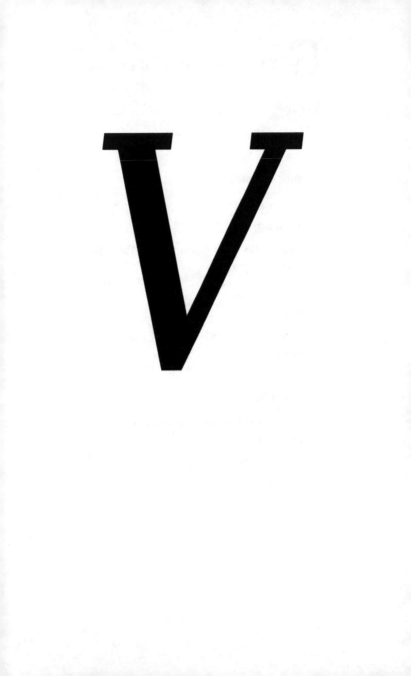

Vanity

The quicksand of reason.

George Sand

Other people's pride.

Sacha Guitry

Vegetarians

People who look enough like their food to be classed as cannibals.

Finley Peter Dunne

Venice

Like eating an entire box of chocolate liqueurs at one go.

Truman Capote

Verbal Contract

Something that's not worth the paper it's written on.

Samuel Goldwyn

Vice

A creature of such hideous mien that the more you see it, the better you like it.

Finley Peter Dunne

Its own reward.

Quentin Crisp

Victory

Something that has a hundred fathers – but defeat is an orphan.

Galeazzo Ciano

Violence

The repartee of the illiterate.

Alan Brien

Virgins

Frozen assets.

Clare Boothe Luce

Virtue

Only vices in disguise.

Duc de La Rochefoucauld

The Trade Unionism of the married.

George Bernard Shaw

The avoidance of vices that do not attract us.

Robert Lynd

Insufficient temptation.

George Bernard Shaw

Its own disappointment.

Philip Moeller

Vocation

Any badly-paid job which someone has taken out of choice.

Mike Barfield

Vulgarity

Simply the conduct of other people.

Oscar Wilde

The garlic in the salad of taste.

Cyril Connolly

The rich man's modest contribution to democracy.

Samuel Johnson

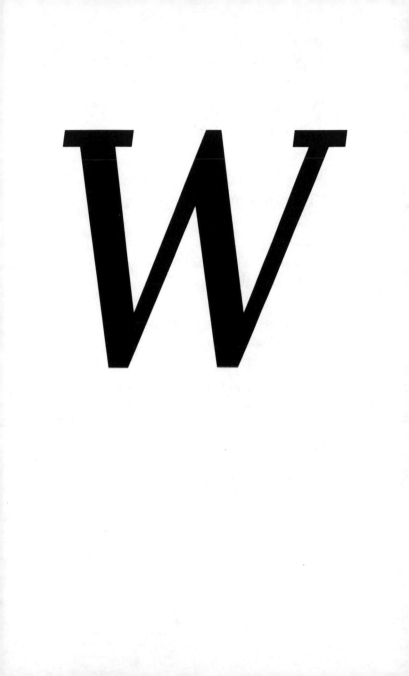

Waiting

The opposite of talking.

Fran Lebowitz

Wales

The land of my fathers – and my fathers can have it.

Dylan Thomas

A country where the only concession to gaiety is a striped shroud.

Gwyn Thomas

A country full of ugly chapels, hidden money, psalm-singing...and rain.

Norman Lewis

A country where Sunday starts early, and lasts several years.

Peg Bracken

War

Capitalism with the gloves off.

Tom Stoppard

A luxury which only the small nations can afford.

Hannah Arendt

The unfolding of miscalculations.

Barbara Tuchman

An organised bore.

Oliver Wendell Holmes Jnr

The national industry of Prussia.

Comte de Mirabeau

Like love, something that always finds a way.

Bertolt Brecht

Something that frequently begins ten years
before the first shot is fired.

Kevin Casey

Water

What fish fuck in.

W.C. Fields

Water Closet

Like the harp, essentially a solo instrument.

Robert Reisner

Wealth

Any income that's at least $100 more a year
than the income of one's wife's sister's husband.

H.L. Mencken

A power usurped by the few to compel the
many to labour for their benefit.

Percy Bysshe Shelley

Wedding

A funeral where you can smell your own
flowers.

Eddie Cantor

The day of a man's life when he realises that he
can't face another date with a legal secretary
who wants to be a nightclub comedienne.

Henny Youngman

Wedlock

A type of lock that is most easily undone
nowadays.

Mike Barfield

Weed

A plant whose virtues have not yet been
discovered.

Ralph Waldo Emerson

Well-adjusted Executive

One whose intake of pep pills overbalances his consumption of tranquillisers just enough to leave him sufficient energy for his weekly visit to the psychiatrist.

Arthur Motley

Welsh, The

An impotent people, sick with inbreeding, worrying the carcass of an old song.

R.S. Thomas

A people who are insistent that local names must not be pronounced as they are spelt.

John Tickner

Westernisation

Big increase in street crime.

John Koski

Whiskey

The most popular of the cold cures that don't work.

Leonard Rossiter

White House, The

The finest jail in the world.

Harry S. Truman

Wickedness

A myth invented by good people to account for the curious attractiveness of others.

Oscar Wilde

Wife

A woman who tries to turn an old rake into a lawn-mower.

Jack Benny

Winter

The season when we try to keep the house as hot as it was in summer, when we complained about the heat.

Herbert Prochnow

Wisdom

The art of knowing what to overlook.

William James

Knowing you can't be wise.

Paul Engle

Wisecracking

Calisthenics with words.

Dorothy Parker

Wit

The rarest quality to be met with among people of education.

William Hazlitt

The salt of conversation, not the food.

William Hazlitt

Wives

Young men's mistresses, companions for middle age, and old men's nurses.

Francis Bacon

Woman

A thing of beauty and an expense forever.

Leopold Fechtner

A diet waiting to happen.

Serena Gray

God's second mistake.

Friedrich Nietzsche

Women

The only exploited group in history who have been idealised into powerlessness.

Erica Jong

People who should be obscene and not heard.

John Lennon

People who give themselves to God when the devil wants nothing more to do with them.

Sophie Arnould

People who like to sit down with trouble as if it were knitting.

Ellen Glasgow

Those who add zest to the unlicensed hours.

Allen D. Thomas

Words

The small change of thought.

Jules Renard

The great foes of reality.

Joseph Conrad

Work

The refuge of those who have nothing better to do.

Oscar Wilde

The province of cattle.

Dorothy Parker

What expands so as to fill the time available for its completion.

C. Northcote Parkinson

The only really dirty four-lettered word in the language.

Abbie Hoffman

The curse of the drinking classes.

Oscar Wilde

World, The

A nice place to visit, but I wouldn't want to live there.

Arlo Guthrie

Worry

Interest paid on trouble before it falls due.

Hal Roach

Writer

Someone who can make a riddle out of an answer.

Karl Kraus

Someone for whom writing is more difficult than it is for other people.

Thomas Mann

Somebody a little below a clown and a little above a trained seal.

John Steinbeck

The Faust of modern society.

Boris Pasternak

A frustrated actor who recites his lines in the hidden auditorium of his skull.

Rod Sterling

Writing

Busy idleness.

Johann Wolfgang von Goethe

What keeps me from believing everything I read.

Gloria Steinem

The hardest work in the world not involving heavy lifting.

Pete Hamill

The hardest way to earn a living, with the possible exception of wrestling alligators.

Olin Miller

The only profession where no one considers you ridiculous if you earn no money.

Jules Renard

The process of staring at a blank sheet of paper until drops of blood form on your forehead.

Gene Fowler

Trivial personalities decomposing in the eternity of print.

Virginia Woolf

Turning one's worst moments into money.

J.P. Donleavy

Not a profession, but a vocation of unhappiness.

Georges Simenon

The process of putting one's obsessions in order.

Jean Grenier

Xerox

A trademark for a photocopying device that can make rapid reproductions of human error perfectly.

Merle Meacham

Youngsters

People who brighten up a home – because they leave the lights on everywhere.

Laurence Peter

Youth

The period when a boy knows everything but how to make a living.

Carey McWilliams

A disease from which we all recover.

Dorothy Fuldheim

Zeal

A nervous disorder afflicting the young and inexperienced.

Ambrose Bierce

Zoo

A place devised for animals to study the habits of human beings.

Oliver Herford

Index